Daniel Casper von Lohenstein's
HISTORICAL TRAGEDIES

Daniel Casper von Lohenstein's
HISTORICAL TRAGEDIES

Gerald Ernest Paul Gillespie

Columbus, Ohio
Ohio State University Press

PREFACE

TREATMENTS of the Thirty Years' War, the epoch of absolutism, and the development of authoritarianism have contributed considerably to a growing interest in German seventeenth-century literature. Much investigation during the last fifty years has doubtless also been stimulated by debate among art historians and musicologists about the "Baroque." What this term means for art or music is still moot, and, as recent studies show, what it signifies for literature is cloudy indeed.

Within the limited scope of this book, the "Baroque" is not an important subject, nor a very useful word. I hope to provide a coherent picture of the dramatist Lohenstein, and, therefore, a fresh interpretation of specific works which are part of his artistic age. A new look at actual texts, without reference to any intellectual construct existing outside them, seems in order —more especially because we have inherited most of our generalizations from the eighteenth and nineteenth centuries.

I am not attempting to write historical scholarship but a work of criticism, which leaves out anything, however important, that does not bear on its unified argument. The point of departure is the question what the playwright says and in what form, rather than whether his statement is "good" or "bad" art, or typically "Baroque," according to preconceived standards. Hence the deliberately pedestrian arrangement of chapter topics around analyses of individual plays.

The tacit assumption of the book is that each play obeys the laws of its own being as a unique work of art—whether good or bad, successful or unsuccessful—and that by searching out its fundamental conception we can better understand its style and form. Of course, peculiarities of style and form also manifest deeper impulses in the artist's total productivity and in his relationship to his own condition and times. The creative impulses underlying groups of plays are our primary business; their dependence upon formal modes of expression developed by his age is secondary. That is, the approach is from the works to the times—with recognition of a vital interplay.

Lohenstein's period and its typical media are not adduced as explanations. Likewise, the biography of the dead artist is here subordinate to the products of creative intellect. As H. D. F. Kitto has said, "Criticism . . . can without discredit begin with what is in the poet's head, without inquiring how it got there" (*Greek Tragedy* [1939]). Disturbed, nevertheless, by traditional German rejection of French classical drama, I have also tried to infer, through attending performances of this related "foreign" theater in Paris, how certain meanings may have gotten into Lohenstein's head, even what the living context of tragedy may have been for a Silesian lawyer in the days of Gryphius. But I omit such historical guesses, because only the particular messages remain and are the proper matter of my monograph.

Naturally, statements by other commentators have induced me to restrict my own. I have endeavored to reiterate only that common ground necessary for comprehensibility and to cite disagreement rather than agreement. My debts are noted more fully in the dissertation on Lohenstein which I presented in August, 1961, at the Ohio State University. I wish to thank Professor Walter Naumann of the Technische Hochschule Darmstadt, formerly of the Ohio State University, for encouragement and criticism of my efforts in this study. The Germanistic Society of America generously awarded the Max Kade Fellowship for 1960–61, allowing me to complete research with access to materials held by German libraries. The University of Southern California has with equal generosity given its support, so that I could revise this essay for presentation to a wider audience.

G. GILLESPIE

Los Angeles, 1963

CONTENTS

Daniel Casper von Lohenstein's
HISTORICAL TRAGEDIES

Chapter One

LOHENSTEIN'S POSITION AS A PLAYWRIGHT

ALTHOUGH considerable is known about Daniel Casper von Lohenstein (1635–83), no adequate biography has yet been written. His life fitted a pattern prevalent in his homeland Silesia, which in the seventeenth century had become an important center of literary activity furthered by the influential ministerial class of the various principalities and cities. The constant turmoil of the Thirty Years' War had quickened a renewal of Roman stoic philosophy among the region's scholars, jurists, and other educated bourgeois. Lohenstein was born into this class as a member of the Protestant Casper family while it was in refuge at Nimptsch. His father, an imperial tax official, was decorated for saving treasury funds under attack. Steeped very early in classical studies as a pupil (1643–51) at the Magdalenaeum, an outstanding humanist gymnasium in Breslau, Lohenstein began to compose poetry of serious tenor in Latin and German and, at the age of fifteen, produced his first play, *Ibrahim Bassa* (1650), for the active school theater. After legal studies at Leipzig and residence at Tübingen, leading to a doctorate (1653), he undertook a journey (1655–56) through Germany, Switzerland, and the Netherlands.

Many exiled Protestants had found a wartime haven in the thriving Dutch nation. Its culture continued to attract Germans, and its universities, principally Leyden, played a large role in mediating newer views in philosophy and art. A fellow Silesian playwright, the great poet Andreas Gryphius (1616–64), had visited the Netherlands and also Paris. Like this forerunner, Lohenstein doubtless experienced in Holland the tragic theater of Jost van den Vondel (1587–1679) and other Dutch imitators of antiquity. The Senecan tradition and English historical plays provided models for the age, which was first and foremost politically oriented. Affairs of state, the play of fortune, and heroic suffering appealed to a public apparently never sated by the contrasting spectacles of greatness and misery. The predominant influence from France was, similarly, a drama of Roman fortitude and sublime ambition, as best represented by the protagonists of Pierre Corneille (1606–84). Southern influence was paramount in contemporary poetics, and Italian and French ideas also affected German literature through Holland, for the Dutch followed in the wake of late Renaissance theoreticians like Julius Caesar Scaliger (1484–1558). The Dutch scholar Daniel Heinsius (1580–1665) was a notable mediator in the flow of concepts of the theater from the Latin nations. We shall soon touch on some of the consequences.

After his return to Silesia, Lohenstein traveled in the course of two years into Styria and Hungary, seeing the borderlands threatened by the Ottoman empire. He entered upon a legal career and served in several capacities in the government of Breslau for most of his mature years. In 1675, he acted as the imperial city's confidential envoy to the Austrian court, and there negotiated a favorable tax treaty which preserved its liberties. For these outstanding services he received the title *Lohenstein,* after a stream on his property. His contemporaries admired him as an able man of affairs and letters, and he won the friendship of the chief Silesian poets. Along with political activity, Lohenstein studied zealously and widely and especially deepened his knowledge of the ancient world. His name became, in fact, synonymous with sententious wisdom, as the title of a posthumous collection of excerpts from his works, *Lohensteinius sententiosus* (1710), demonstrates. A humanist scholar, he documented copiously all the references in his historical tragedies

4

(excluding *Ibrahim Bassa*) and published the annoted works through the printer Fellgibel of Breslau: *Epicharis* (1665), *Agrippina* (1665), *Ibrahim Sultan* (1673), *Cleopatra* (1661; revised edition, 1680), and *Sophonisbe* (1680). All these annotated plays are set in the Mediterranean world and beshadowed by either Roman or Ottoman tyranny; all their title figures are pagan; and only one *(I.S.)* suggests indirectly an opponent Christendom.[1]

Lohenstein's most popular work, the huge polyhistoric compendium *Arminius* (published posthumously, 1689–90), strove to formulate in exemplary fashion all that one should know about history and society. It was an heroic-gallant encyclopedia in fictional form, but of so ambitious a scope that it attempted to revise the picture of German antiquity and destiny. Lohenstein's patriotic reinterpretation of the past cast under shadow the glory of the Romans. All non-Roman heroes, according to the novel, were either Germans, disguised Germans, or German allies, whose genuine virtues stood in clear contrast to the spurious merits of the enemy. Lohenstein projected evident contemporary figures like the Austrian emperor into the ancient heroes who fought Roman duplicity and corruption. He read ideals into the age of Arminius along with political prophecies of his nation's future greatness. This complicated mythology of German history, with attention shifting back and forth between present and past, entertained its public well into the early eighteenth century and became grandsire to countless nationalistic Arminiuses (e.g., Klopstock's, Kleist's, etc.).[2] And Lohenstein's reputation might have survived, greatly diminished but unsullied, had the novel alone represented him. However, with the triumph of Pietism and the rationalist faith in nature, the concepts of "political" and "courtly" man, which Lohenstein united in his works, became increasingly repugnant. Dramas such as Lessing's *Emilia Galotti* (1772) and Schiller's *Kabale*

5

und Liebe (1783) protested against the whole civilization which the Machiavellian courtly era represented, and Lohenstein was swept out upon the Rousseauian tide.

German secular lyricism had already undergone a thorough schooling in the Romance Renaissance models, and the so-called anacreontic and petrarchistic modes were well established in Germany in the first decades of the seventeenth century. From the beginning this worldly poetry showed a tendency toward hyperbole. A late phase, the vogue of manneristic poetry as exemplified by Giambattista Marino (1569–1625), Luis de Góngora (1561–1627), and others, swept Lohenstein's generation. Southern *concettismo* flourished in France for approximately three decades after 1630, although it was already passé in England (John Lyly's *Euphues: The Anatomy of Wit,* published at the end of 1578, launched the vogue of exaggeratedly refined language there much earlier); and a whole style of speech and life called preciosity evolved, whose influence radiated from key salons, such as that of "Sappho," i.e. Mlle de Scudéry. Preciosity did encourage writers to compose psychologistic works with refinement and idealism, but led to excesses. Disdaining ordinary language, the *précieux* often went beyond ordinary logic in their gallant comparisons, sought paraphrases and extended metaphors, and cultivated the striking point which would demonstrate subtle wit. By the end of the century some writers, for example, Christian Wernicke, in his *Ueberschriften oder Epigrammata in kurzen Satyren* (Amsterdam, 1697), already criticised and parodied their forebears. The rhetorical and gallant poets, led by the Silesian Christian Hofmann von Hofmannswaldau (1618–97), were charged with pedantic copying and absurd bombast. If, in a typical Renaissance formula, Lohenstein excused his own writings as a product of leisure hours, amusement for a busy lawyer and scholar, sentimental and enlightened critics soon took him seriously and regarded him as a representative of poetry without genuine feeling. They looked on any coldly rational playing with words as a lewd mockery of the human heart. The discrepancy between seventeenth-century and modern evaluations of Lohenstein is an important fact, attributable in large part to the very different views on art held before and after his death. But, above and beyond the new age's aesthetic requirements, he failed to satisfy its needs for a poetry which expressed faith in a harmonious world order and correspondent qualities of soul.

Lohenstein's poetry, while treating a mixture of themes, is not extensive or of consistent quality. In addition to his translations from Petrarch, Marino, and other Romance poets, his work ranges over pansophic thought, explores his age's anxiety before transitory existence, and glorifies love. As we shall see, the dramas have a similar scope. Least important artistically are his spiritual poems, which combine formulations reminiscent of the theosophist Jakob Böhme (1575–1624) and rationalistic doctrines but lack any deep Christian feeling. Although Lohenstein uses the traditional mystical terminology, speaking of God as the wellspring and ocean of light, his real concern is not with religion at all but rather with reason and its mysterious involvement in the flesh. For example, the poem "Leitung der Vernunft zu der ewigen Zeugung und Menschwerdung des Sohns Gottes" betrays the influence of Cartesian thought; it develops Christ's incarnation into an illustrative metaphor for the coexistence of a corporeal and spiritual universe, as in the line: "Die Seele komme Gott / der Leib dem Viehe gleich."[3] The poet often reflects seventeenth-century mechanistic psychology, the dualistic view of human nature as a conflict between reason and passion. One discovers related dualities in Lohenstein's elegies to parted friends and prominent persons. These poems, very solemn and obsessed with the sense of life's transitoriness, are also his best. The constant emphasis is, however, not on salvation but rather on *fame*, immortality through "greatness of soul." The way to triumph over the human condition is to be resolute, heroic in mind and deed. He regards the magnanimity of those he celebrates, of course, as also moral. But this connection between morality and stature becomes insignificant for certain of his dramatic protagonists who appeal through sheer struggle. Again, the elegies' favorite images have to do with "light," which is of the soul and derives from the stars. It signifies either the workings of the guiding principle of greatness, i.e., reason, or, alternately, the promise of eternity, i.e., renown. Light connects man to the fixed luminaries, to the deathless heroes symbolized by heavenly constellations. Thus, when the poet equates reason with virtue *(Tugend)*, he means manliness, not Christian goodness.

While certain of Lohenstein's poems proclaim the glory of reason, even the necessary tyranny of reason, his love poems, or rather poems about love, indicate belief in another universal principle, an attractive force moving the whole world. Lohenstein's gallant poems often deal with disputes on matters of love and marriage, stress the good of earthly felicity with voluptuous detail, and express pro-feminine sentiments. A neo-Platonic strain can be heard in many of these pieces. The prose poem "Vereinbarung der Sterne und der Gemüther," for example, is an epithalamium in the pagan manner of a Renaissance lyricist like Johannes Secundus (1511–1536) and its philosophic speculation ends with erotic glorification of the natural state in marriage. Lohenstein takes up macrocosmic-microcosmic concepts and posits a correspondence between man and his universe; he acknowledges a vague determinism represented by or in the influence of the stars. But what is more important, he recognizes a correspondence between external and internal charm ("Ein wohlgebildet Leib bewirthet edle Seelen"), a suggestion one finds elsewhere in his works. In celebrating the human body, he mentions a hidden harmony in creatures destined for each other ("die unzertrennlichen

8

Seelen- und Leibes-Verbindung").[4] For a modern reader used
to introspective techniques for exploration of the "inside" of
man, Lohenstein's sententious remarks often obscure his fatalistic tone and attitude. His tendency is to psychologize rather
than moralize, although his language is not confessional but
representative. And many poems, like this epithalamium, suggest a psychological picture of mankind, not identical with, but
at least more related to the Böhmean than Cartesian mode of
thought. Lohenstein's suspicion that body and soul are inter-
related, in a synthesis, has its parallel here in the implied
metaphor of the sexes, which are both antithetical and complementary. Elsewhere he is less sanguine, or is swayed by a more
mechanistic interpretation of life. Some passages in the plays
condemn, others elevate love; it is a central and ambiguous
issue, around which Lohenstein builds much of his plots. Certainly he creates many title heroines in order to reinterpret
love as varied phenomena which are microcosmic manifestations of some macrocosmic principle. As in French classical
drama, love often subserves fate. But, as we shall see, Lohenstein
treats more than sentimentalized passion; for him, fate includes
much more, and the final resolution or synthesis is very
puzzling indeed.

The frivolity of much of gallant lyric in Germany can blind
us to the serious drift in Lohenstein. While seventeenth-century
dualistic psychology seems dominant in his thinking, he never
consistently relegates even carnal love to the irrevocably negative sphere. He may sometimes unmask the dubious attractiveness in the world to show horrors underneath, as in Gryphius'
drama. But Lohenstein ultimately leaves open the question
about beauty and acknowledges a genuine mystery in the non-
rational forces which drive the universe. He cannot, therefore,
be judged adequately on the basis of seventeenth-century
religiosity, even though his century brought forth great religious
expression, and least of all from a narrowly Protestant stand-

point. Although Breslau was Protestant, the philosophic and literary currents of the Counter Reformation, transmitted by Vienna, flowed through it. Lohenstein's worldly-wise formulations derive mainly from Romance sources, such as the Jesuit philosopher Balthasar Gracián's (1584–1658) *Político*, which Lohenstein translated into German (1679). Mystical writing and Protestant lyric flourished side by side with courtly and gallant genres from southern Catholic lands. As much as Lohenstein was open to the influence of both religious confessions, he was not moved by Christian thought any more than by the record of the ancients and by new rationalistic currents. And we shall discuss this secular orientation again soon in regard to the dramas. His humanistic outlook, eclectic receptivity to foreign influences, and poetic tendencies mark him as a follower of Martin Opitz (1597–1639).

Opitz based his composite poetics, the influential *Buch von der deutschen Poeterey* (1624), on neo-classical concepts and the examples of French and Italian literature. He urged the German nation to emulate these, as had the Dutch already, and to attain thereby a stature equivalent to that won by the great cultures of Romance tongue. His literary contemporaries were eager for such a task, and were actually already working toward the goal of his program, which was to break with native traditions that lacked prestige and to Europeanize German letters. Opitz himself contributed, as models, both original works and translations in many genres, such as the didactic pastoral *Hercinie* (1630); the first German opera, *Daphne* (1627); and Sophocles' *Antigone* (1636), rendered, however, in the style of Seneca. In spite of his shortcomings, his imitative enthusiasm and that of numerous other men of letters persevered in the terrible crisis of the Thirty Years' War; their accomplishment is considerable, seen against this background. A cultural society, the Fruchtbringende Gesellschaft, founded in 1617 in imitation of the Accademia della Crusca (1582) in

Florence, already was striving for reform of German poetry according to classical and Romance models, and other groups soon followed its lead. Though their view of the poetic office was based on Latin tradition, the humanists participated in the immense task of translation, assimilation, and imitation of respected "modern" authorities, as had the Pléiade in France in the sixteenth century, and with similar objectives. Since the main concern of the German reform movement was at first to practice foreign techniques in order to achieve a higher level of local artistic capability, many experiments had to make headway against native traditions, sometimes with unhappy results.

And often, as for the drama, the reform critics like Opitz had very little profound or unique to offer, and simply transcribed a set of Renaissance predilections which were superimposed on existing popular theater. The native stage's four-beat line *(Knittelvers)*, inherited from the Middle Ages, was driven out and replaced by the French alexandrine, which gave way in turn in the eighteenth century to a second foreign borrowing, English blank verse, an ultimately more successful venture. The generic pre-eminence of tragedy was not yet established. In the fifth chapter of his treatise, Opitz considered the epic as the most important and difficult art form; the tragedy, to be sure, was of similar majestic tone and excluded persons of low rank and "simple" actions. Royal deeds, powerful emotions, great suffering were the stuff of tragedy—thus pathos in its basic sense. Unfortunately, this definition of pathetic drama was interpreted crudely in the vein of the popular theater (" . . . von Königlichem willen, Todtschlägen, verzweiffelungen, Kinder- und Vätermörden, brande, blutschanden, kriege und auffruhr, klagen, heulen, seuffzen und dergleichen . . ."). Opitz covered little new ground in introducing his translation of Seneca's *Die Trojanerinnen* (1619) and defining the tragedy, after Epictetus, as a mirror of those whose existence was based on Fortune; the show of political and human catastrophes, while stirring our sympathies, was to fortify us against suffering. The intended effect was, then, primarily the rehardening of stoic constancy through examples, and only secondarily the experiencing of pity.[5]

As Bruno Markwardt notes, here one aspect of catharsis, the ancient educative experience—stoic apathy—proved stronger than the Christian principle, whereas the Enlightenment emphasized the theory of sympathy.[6] Since several waves of theatrical reform (Gottsched, Lessing) finally made the divergence of aesthetic attitudes practically unbridgeable, it is useful to recall the state of drama in Lohenstein's time and to sketch the changes which were conducive to this rupture with the past. Eighteenth-century objections to him were, of course, partly a second phase in the rejection of the supposedly disordered, inferior German past in favor of a "European" classicism (Gottsched), but also partly a final rejection of whatever seemed to represent the older French influence in favor of a humane, sentimental ideal of human nature as exemplified by English models (Lessing).[7]

The Protestant Reformation had changed the dramatic climate of Germany. First of all, the medieval mystery and Passion plays receded further and further south into the mountains and virtually disappeared as a national tradition. The vernacular Protestant drama, spreading among the bourgeoisie who had formerly participated in these outdoor community productions, began itself to decline by the end of the sixteenth century. The first modest indoor stages were in the humanist schools, which used plays to train their pupils in Latin and to edify. These aims fitted the Lutheran program, so that the schools were encouraged to develop German dramatic exercises. The old Protestant academic theater remained active in Latin, too, especially in Strassburg, where it continued into the seventeenth century. The rising Jesuit drama succeeded, however, in gaining a hold in many of the humanist schools, and the Counter Reformation had a major influence upon the vernacular stage by the time of the Thirty Years' War. Among the outstanding Jesuit playwrights were Jakob Bidermann (1578–1639) and Nikolaus Avancini (1612–86), and doubtless the most famous Jesuit play is the former's *Cenodoxus* (1602). The center of gravity for this mainly Latin propagandistic theater was the Bavarian–Austrian area. As in the humanist drama, its purpose was educational and motivational; and theories of rhetoric governed its poetics. Because, however, it spread during a later phase of theatrical development, it employed all the techniques of the newer, illusory stage already perfected in Italy, with changeable scenery, perspective, and machinery, in order to achieve effects such as visions, visitations, etc., and it tended to present intellectual issues with the pomp and splendor of opera. Catholic ritualism favored the adaptation of traits which satisfied the popular need for spectacle. The opera itself, which Italian humanists had originally developed to be a revival of ancient tragedy with its musical choruses, made devastating inroads upon, and diverted the support of the monied classes from, grand theater. This socio-economic factor contributed to the serious lag in the development of the German stage.

Popular usages had survived from the Middle Ages, as in the Shrovetide plays, fool plays, and joke plays *(Schwänke)* of Hans Sachs (1494–1576), who modified their harshness and also introduced classical lore as subject matter. Like his forerunner Sachs, the Nürnberger dramatist Jakob Ayrer (1543–1605) utilized the older forms, including *Knittelvers* (four-beat line), and a similarly wide range of materials drawn from the *Decameron*, chapbooks, etc. His fool plays, histories, and tragedies also borrowed considerably from the drama of England, and he wrote a number of musical interludes in the English tradition *(Singspiele)*. Groups of strolling players, because of their origin called "English comedians," had come to the Continent in the sixteenth century, introducing a style of acting which tended toward an often brutal naturalism. Gradually their personnel became German, and also their language. The repertory consisted of morality and biblical plays, suiting the declining Protestant taste, but principally it was made up of English histories, tragedies, and comedies; by 1630, French and Italian pieces were integrated into the stock. Since the clown was especially popular, a company usually grouped itself around a chief actor who, as in the *commedia dell' arte*, played extempore a fixed character, with names such as Jean Bossuet or Pickelhäring. Like the Jesuits, the English comedians created visual, affective spectacles. They often staged gruesome displays—executions, tortures, apparitions, aggressive devils, and the like—to shake the audience. Duke Heirich Julius of Brunswick (1564–1613) patronized the English comedians and tried to develop and raise their art in his own plays. English comedy reached its zenith between the turn of the century and the start of the Thirty Years' War. Again like the Jesuits, companies of players gravitated to the courts, the centers of power, although, unlike the powerful order, they continued on the whole to be wandering troupes without a permanent court connection. Count Moritz of Hessen (1572–1632), another patron–playwright, founded Germany's first fixed theater for them in 1604–5.

The pejorative term *Haupt- und Staatsaktion* designates a play with mixture of subjects and styles, especially alternation of clowning with a bloodthirsty or solemn progress, characteristic of Germany's popular theatrical entertainment in the late seventeenth century. The clown ran through the scenes, commenting bizarrely on the action and doing stunts, and was often the actual center of attention. But there was usually a main plot *(Haupt-)* portraying the affairs of politically important and splendidly attired figures of the great world *(Staats-)*, frequently based on historical personages. Lohenstein's plays sometimes wallow in cruel naturalism and certainly employ this pomp of state, but their serious tone is closer to that of the humanistic school drama and Jesuit tradition. Unlike Gryphius, he never even attempted a single comedy. Despite the total absence of clowning, his work was nevertheless associated by historical proximity with "impure" drama and its bombast and disorder. Since he was also the antithesis of a poet of faith, indeed manifested a *skeptical* rationalism, his failure to conform to the refined criteria for drama at the end of the century seemed doubly blameworthy. The greater freedom of form, also the stoic harshness of heroic themes, of Corneille declined in influence in France during the second half of the seventeenth century. England underwent a similar change of mood, accepting the pruned, elegant heroic plays of John Dryden (1631–1700), the lofty languishing of *All for Love* (1678), in place of Shakespeare's magnificently sprawling *Antony and Cleopatra* (ca. 1606–7). The strict French rules, which required scenic simplicity, verisimilitude, ennobling of protagonists through the use of *alter egos,* and a purified vocabulary, made an impression on Germany only after Lohenstein's death.

The next major reformer, Johann Christian Gottsched (1700–66), defender of this pruned classical ideal, was hostile toward pastoral, heroic, and courtly poetry in the Italian mode, which he considered lascivious, and toward similar "excesses" in the favored French. In drama, all violence, horror, and eroticism was to be kept in the wings, not played. The unities enshrined by the French Academy and elevated by the usage of Jean Racine (1639–99) were recommended to a later age unable, because of its bourgeois spirit, to understand this severe aristocratic formalism. Eventually French and English bourgeois subjects were represented by followers of the reform, as in works by Johann Elias Schlegel (1718–49). Gottsched also attacked the pathos of Senecan tragedy, so important for the humanists; actually he wanted to continue the Renaissance tradition of grandiloquent expression of suffering, but opposed exaggerated conceits and bombast in favor of a "natural" language. Thus he consigned Hofmannswaldau and Lohenstein to one poetic camp, but a purer Gryphius and his kind to a counterposition—a contrast which occurs in all criticism afterward to the present.[8] He singled out Lohenstein as the bombastic German par excellence in the theater.[9]

The sentimental doctrine of the "beautiful soul" was developing simultaneously with the new trend in aesthetics which emphasized naturalness. For the seventeenth century, nature did not yet represent anything moral, although there are already a few suggestions of Rousseauian thought even in Lohenstein, as well as in pietistic poetry, notably, the Königsberger circle (Robert Roberthin, Simon Dach, *et al.*). Very often poets saw just the opposite, an inimical natural world which meant perilous travail for man, who fought to rescue his soul from engulfment in bestial chaos. But optimistic rationalism, with its view of a perfectly designed universe, and pietistic faith interacted eventually to create trust in nature as a harmonious order; Gottfried Wilhelm Leibniz' (1646–1716) doctrine of theodicy provided a systematic framework for the emerging belief. Appealing literature from England, such as the works of James Thomson (1700–48) and Edward Young (1681–1765), already went beyond ordinary rationalistic sentiments in exploring the beauty and meaning of nature; it held the deepest significance for inward life. In general, the Germans discovered in English literature a counterforce against the long, frustrating dominion of French influence. The rejection of courtly civilization and, correspondingly, the interest in nature, natural morality, and the sentiments of ordinary life developed most rapidly in the Swiss area. Its poet Albrecht von Haller (1708–77) in German and the philosopher Jean–Jacques Rousseau (1712–78) in French vigorously forwarded the newer ideals of natural humanity. Its leading critics, Johann Jakob Bodmer (1698–1783) and Johann Jakob Breitinger (1701–76), rejected even Gottsched's reformed drama, championed English authors as examplars of true poetry, and made devastating attacks upon Lohenstein and the courtly-gallant Silesian school. Bodmer wrote an entertainingly severe parody of *Arminius* in part three, discourse fourteen, of *Discourse der Mahlern* (1721–23). The novel was still being read and was republished as late as 1731, but Lohenstein's works could not survive beyond the fourth decade. His tragedies—unplayed but still in print—went into eclipse after Breitinger's biting commentary scorning them as disordered bombast and depraved fluctuation between extremes:

> Wann ich nur an Lohensteins Trauerspiele gedencke, so überfällt mich Frost und Eckel, der geduldigste Mensch, der nicht zugleich dumm ist, möchte über dem Lesen dieser Tragödien die Schwindsucht bekommen. Da findet man nichts anderes als eine ungestaltete und ungeordnete Materie, einen Haufen verworrener Begebenheiten, wo weder Ort, noch Zeit, noch Wohlstand beobachtet ist. . . . Wenn er bald in lauter Gleichnissen und Metaphorn mit sich selbst zancket, bald um eine Schöne von seiner eigenen Schöpfung in Schwulst und Wahnwitz buhlet, bald die verborgensten und seltensten Wunder der Natur mit einem Doctormässigen Ernst erkläret, wenn er plötzlich, wie in einer Verzückung, aus sich selbst geräth, und über die Wolcken fliegt, und im Augenblick wieder so tiefe fällt, dass er mit kindischen Sprüchwörtern, spitzfindigen Spielen, schliessenden Gleichnissen und dergleichen ohne Mass um sich wirft. Die höchste Hitze und der höchste Frost wechseln bey ihm ab, ein Kennzeichen des äussersten Verderbnisses in der Schreibart, wie der schwersten Krankheit in dem menschlichen Leib. In allen diesen Stücken hat Andr. Gryphius vor ihm nicht viel zum Voraus, ausgenommen dass seine Personen in einer menschlichern Sprache reden. . . . [10]

Indeed, while Gryphius managed to maintain a small credit, it was little enough that Breitinger granted.

It is interesting to note that critics for the natural frequently disapproved, with similar terminology, of other artists from the seventeenth century, many of whom, like Gryphius, have since been rehabilitated, usually because of their religious intensity whose appeal could resurge. Lohenstein lacks such appeal; he has no spiritual merits and stands apart from any of his sincerely religious contemporaries. In the *Critischer Musikus* (Leipzig; May 14, 1737), Johann Adolph Scheibe nevertheless turned all the complaints about seventeenth-century poetry against the music of Johann Sebastian Bach (1685–1750), who would be a "wonder," were he only not "bombastic," "obscure," "artificial," striving "against reason"—like Lohenstein:

> Dieser grosse Mann würde die Bewunderung ganzer Nationen sein, wenn er mehr Annehmlichkeit hätte und wenn er nicht seinen Stücken durch ein schwülstiges und verworrenes Wesen das Natürliche entzöge und ihre Schönheit durch allzugrosse Kunst verdunkelte. . . . Alle Manieren, alle kleinen Verzierungen drückt er mit eigentlichen Noten aus, und das entzieht seinen Stücken nicht nur die Schönheit der Harmonie, sondern es macht auch den Gesang durchaus unvernehmlich. Alle Stimmen sollen miteinander und mit der gleichen Schwierigkeit arbeiten, und mann erkennt darunter keine Hauptstimme. Kurz: er ist in der Musik dasjenige, was ehemals Herr von Lohenstein in der Poesie war. Die Schwülstigkeit hat beide von dem Natürlichen auf das Künstliche und von dem Erhabenen auf das Dunkle geführt; und man bewundert an beiden die beschwerliche Arbeit und eine ausnehmende Mühe, die doch vergebens angewandt ist, weil sie wider die Vernunft streitet.

Without presuming, as does Scheibe's critique, to compare Lohenstein and Bach, we may legitimately accept the rejected categories of the "artificial" and "obscure," traits the new age could not tolerate, as indicative of a past impulse in art. And indeed, Lohenstein's pagan heroes exemplify fateful yearnings and strivings, his polyhistorical interest exhibits a dark side. The final suicide of protagonists is but one irrational brush stroke in the playwright's picture of the world. We shall examine these features at some length, since they have disturbed generations of critics.

Gryphius' dramas treat terrible outrages against noble victims who, in a lesser degree than their tormentors, evince irrational longings; but his martyr-heroes never technically commit suicide, rather they accept death at the hands of others in defense of their faith. Only their goodness provokes the world's envy and malice. Lohenstein's protagonists, however, are active and violent, even when on the "good" side, and the values they uphold are rarely Christian. Thus most commentators contrast the playwright Gryphius' religiosity and "inwardness" with Lohenstein's lack of these qualities. The Goethean epoch could accept Gryphius because he seemed to offer, despite rhetoric and gruesomeness at times, a moral harmony, the attributes of beauty of soul then so prized. Although the Romantics were quite independent in their evaluations of the German past, Tieck, too, expressed disturbance over Lohenstein's shadow side in the commentary to accompany *Ibrahim Bassa* in the collection *Deutsches Theater* (1817).[11] The tendency set in to approve of only this play because it was close to Gryphius. And thus W. A. Passow, in 1852; F. Bobertag, in 1875; O. Muris, in 1911; H. Cysarz, in 1924; J. Nadler, in 1931; and W. P. Friederich, in 1935, preferred it for its inward, pious, simple features. Imitating the dicta of Bodmer and Breitinger, the nineteenth century magnified the image of the perverse, cynical Lohenstein, and this lexicon reputation reached into the twentieth century. Although Felix Bobertag edited Lohenstein's *Cleopatra* for the series *Deutsche National–Litteratur* (1885), he introduced it with apologies as a kind of study in pathology and stressed only the failure of the seventeenth century to comprehend the tragic.[12]

The old note of moral aspersion reappeared with full vigor in Herbert Cysarz' book *Deutsche Barock–Dichtung* (Leipzig,

1924); the chapter entitled "Theatralik" directed withering critical blasts against Lohenstein for parading costumed pathos upon a stage without purpose, unlike Gryphius, for offering only a berserk spectacle. As late a commentator as Erik Lunding acknowledged agreement with Cysarz' concept of empty theatricality, but admitted that Lohenstein's drama was more effective and suited for the stage than Gryphius'.[13] This same tribute is found among the less flattering remarks by Werner Paul Friederich; his article, also influenced by Cysarz, redefined the moral cleavage between the hateful and beautiful souls of the seventeenth century, the sheep and the goats. Its title, "From Ethos to Pathos: The Development from Gryphius to Lohenstein," summarized the antithesis once more, a polarity that allegedly made Lohenstein's work come out a twisted exaggeration of the very style and subject matter which demonstrate Gryphius' greatness:

> The main difference between the two dramatists lies in the shifting from a stern Ethos to a sensational Pathos. Gryphius wanted to teach; his preface to the tragedies, speaking of the horrors of war and of the vanity of men, emphasizes that point. He creates heroes whose life is no problem at all for them, but a categorical imperative (Papinianus). Such pure souls then, only rarely a prey of despair, become his mouthpiece in his preachings against the wickedness of tyrants and in his exultations of Christian courage. Lohenstein, apart from his moralizing platitudes imitated from Seneca, has no such strength of religion and character. Both authors represent the two extreme forms of thought of a century which oscillated between religious devotion and coarse sensuality. If, in Gryphius, we eliminate his high ethical purpose, then we see nothing but an empty shell of hideousness and disgust. Such are, to put it brutally, the works of Lohenstein. Rationalism could destroy the religious drama, that is true; on the other hand, there existed no further possibilities of development for such a Senecan shell and the dramas of Lohenstein died of their own excesses.[14]

But with a strange sort of reasoning, Friederich acknowledged that Lohenstein's unethical and empty theater, rather than Gryphius', really presents a dramatic conflict:

> Gryphius' tragedies were elegies, not dramas in the proper sense of the word, for the ultimate fate of the heroes was sealed from the very beginning, and they, full of religious fervor and Christian stoicism, did not stage a fight for their lives. Lohenstein's dramas, however, by their very emphasis on psychology and intrigue, become full of life and passion. . . .
> He has particularly created gigantic women who in their wild desires are more dynamic and human than the proudly resigned martyrs of Gryphius. Women like Agrippina or Cleopatra are not bound by religious dogma; their fate is within themselves and they act accordingly.[15]

The original arguments on which later criticism was based had stressed Lohenstein's failure to present a more human and inward sort of heroic figure. Now this argument produces, after two hundred years, an interesting contradiction in the system of values which supposedly sundered him from Gryphius. Lohenstein's characters, though not pure souls, have—so Friederich implies—problematic lives. The playwright who supposedly distorts drama into mere theatricality seems to do this by dealing with life and passion. In Gryphian drama, "fate" is only the foreseen issue of a play founded like the world stage upon a bedrock of Christian belief, whereas Lohensteinian "fate" emerges as an inherent challenge out of one's role, so that it provokes an active and even desperate response by the individual whom it touches.

Most critics subordinate "pathos," the often hysterical expression of desperation in Lohenstein, as "theatricality." Friederich, nonetheless, thinks of this theatricality as "rationalism," and passes over its very peculiarity—that it often has a frenetic pitch. Although he recognizes the suspicious fact that feminine protagonists characterize its vitality, he continues to work with the unrewarding polarity of a rational (here implicitly negative) versus religious (implicitly positive) impulse in two opposed types of seventeenth-century dramaturgy. A more accurate definition of Lohenstein's position would have to take into account that, like Gryphius, he was drawn to the rhetorical, "operatic" expression of deep anxieties about existence but allow without reproach that his "pathos" expressed secular concerns. To be sure, all the issues were not yet clear, but Lohenstein was groping toward some explanation of man's captivity in time, of his condition as a biological and political creature, other than the Christian. Although we may conclude finally that Lohenstein is of lesser rank as a playwright, when judged aesthetically and totally, the fact he was Germany's first serious, secular tragedian after the Middle Ages is most exciting and worth closer study. Naturally, terms such as "reason," different in meaning for various men and epochs, present difficulties. Since seventeenth-century concepts differ from those of German classicism, one cannot assess an author's commitment to "reason" until one knows whether to talk about "moral reason," "tyrannical reason," or some other sort, be it even "the reason of unreason." For example, when Corneille's title hero in *Horace* (1640) kills his own sister out of Roman piety in order to defend the state, he demonstrates heroic virtue—which horrified the audiences of the day; his combination of *raison d'état* and diamondhard *ratio* may impress us, too, on different or similar grounds, as madness. Thus, for the purposes of this essay, words like "rational," "natural," "divine," and the like do not imply moral judgments; and wherever no epochal context is given or assumed for such terms, the present-day, descriptive meaning applies.

Significantly, the eighteenth century worried both that Lohenstein strove against reason and that he was coldly rational. This persistent contradiction, which followed as much from inconsistencies in eighteenth-century thought about reason as from critical observation, needs to be explained; but it needs to be explained in regard to Lohenstein's picture of humanity and history. The roles which the dramatist conceived determine in large measure the dramatic climate of his world. Heroines and courtesans command his stage. Lohenstein's plays do not take place in a pleasant, calm, and moral nature but in the cold marble palaces of the great, who are engaged in a brutal power struggle. Yet constantly he returns to the theme of erotic magnificence and beauty, to a feminine monumentality. On the one hand, passion, charm—all that is provocatively attractive in the world—threaten the stability of human existence which only cunning can guide, so his dramas seem to say. On the other hand, he frequently glorifies the figures who ostensibly are intended as warning examples. This puzzling situation interested a few critics toward the end of the nineteenth century. Although uncertain as to their grounds, they wanted to clear Lohenstein's name from complete scholarly stigmatization. August Kerkhoffs in his book *Daniel Casper von Lohensteins Trauerspiele* (Paderborn, 1877) and Conrad Müller in his *Beiträge zum Leben und Dichten Daniel Caspers von Lohenstein* (Breslau, 1882) blazed a new path with analyses of *Cleopatra*. In the twentieth century Oswald Muris ranked *Cleopatra* next to *Ibrahim Bassa*.[16] Walter Martin in turn saw Cleopatra as Lohenstein's most impressive and successful figure.[17] Max Otto Katz regarded *Cleopatra* and *Sophonisbe* as the epitomes of his art, the latter as "the most mature drama," and tried to explain theatrical excesses.[18] Starting from the assumption that Lohenstein, very realistically oriented, created gigantic villains in order to expose human corruption, Katz concluded that he freed his imagination, perversely and without hypocrisy, to present his vision. Lohenstein was thus evaluated as creator of a psychology of sin and vice, derived from the seventeenth-century view of man as a creature of passions.

Willi Flemming's edition of *Sophonisbe* for the series *Deutsche Literatur* (1931) helped solidify the new interest, and established the African plays' superiority. Laetitia Brede saw the three heroines, Epicharis, Cleopatra, and Sophonisbe, in ascending order, as great tragic personalities and their dramas as expressions of Lohenstein's "hopeless fatalism." [19] Despite Lunding's predilection for "inwardness," he treated both Gryphius and Lohenstein as serious dramatists with coherent world-views and preferred, as had Brede, the plays about the three heroines. Although no one undertook an extensive analysis of the Lohensteinian heroine in the trammels of fate, her vital struggle had generated a more positive attitude toward the dramatist. Fritz Schaufelberger decided, however, that Lohenstein's best figures lacked "form" and remained "mere mask," that the threat to them was "superficial"; because there was no basis of necessity for conflict, such as the metaphysical grounds in Gryphius, Lohenstein could not achieve true tragedy.[20] This opinion clashed with Wolfgang Kayser's partial but brilliant commentary, which defined non-Christian metaphysical grounds, "an ideal nexus," "fate," as the "deepest content" of *Sophonisbe*.[21]

Klaus Günther Just interpreted character and plot motivation as the interplay of two "energies," aptly called "erotic" and "political"; related this duality, useful for understanding the simpler level of "Baroque" psychology, to European theater of the age; but really failed to define Lohenstein's pessimistic rationalism.[22] For, although Lohenstein may be concerned less with absolute norms than with natural laws, Gryphius, too, portrays man as a political creature captive in the human condition without committing outrage against sentimental principles. Lohenstein's offense is to have seen natural laws, which were not necessarily moral, and triumphs of reason, which appeared most unnatural. Gryphius still represents a medieval view of life in which everything relates to God, so that his often agonized scorn for earthly existence befits a total commitment to salvation. Lohenstein, the first modern German dramatist, draws many protagonists who care only for the glory of the world. And therefore (to speak with Friederich and the eighteenth century), he lacks strength of religion and character, in so far as, and in the way that, his stage creations lack these qualities; he is no longer interested in the explanatory duality of God and world, but in the unsafe plurality of motions within the human psyche. Actually, of the many recognizable sets of impulses (e.g., "erotic," "political"), none adequately encompasses the new vision, no duality is final. Lohenstein seems occasionally to regard the human problem as one of reconciling reason, intellect, and ambitious endeavor with the passions; one solution is through exercise of sheer will power, through tyrannical and *not* moral reason, as we see represented in tough Romans like Scipio. But just as often in the dramatic microcosm, the court of any given period, the actors are both governed by Machiavellian expediency and led by conflicting emotions within themselves toward tragic failure. The circumstances for each actor are complex and beyond control, belonging mysteriously to vaster combinations of events and conditions in the historical process. Sometimes the actor (Sophonisbe, Cleopatra) also stands for a whole civilization, so that the individual's story widens into historical vision—the witnessing of nemesis for superpersonal entities.

As Kayser suspected, the resolving concept, Fate, is important. In Lohenstein's drama it transcends all simple dualities, such as love-politics, flesh-spirit, passion-reason, or others. These all apply to the unfolding of the great drama on the world stage, and an isolated conflict may be comprehensible in terms of antitheses, but no greater or lesser resolution is. Any story from the chronicle of time is a subordinate detail in the larger process of synthesis; as in Christian theater of the age, any particular history fits into a grander scheme and the whole "Story" implies "Authorship." We might apply Hegelian terms, not surprisingly, and say that fate is a dialectical principle, the *ultima ratio* in place of God, even though Lohenstein never sharply delineates any secular, versus theological, view; the type of thought epitomized in Böhme's theosophy is the evident ancestor of German mystagogic historicism. But it is better to relate Lohensteinian fate *(Verhängnis)* to his kind of world-stage. If we oversimplify, we see that Gryphius regards nature as a jungle but, with religious conviction, takes refuge in an inward, pure humanity; and that sentimental rationalism, accepting this inner life and some very real evidences of mankind's spiritual evolution, attempts idealistically to make this garden of moral nature congruent with nature as a whole. Lohenstein acknowledges a spiritual realm and nobler humanity —but as a mere clearing in the inexorable jungle; and Gryphius' God is no longer the author and authority here, intervening to redeem the frightful and/or heroic show. Fortune in Lohenstein's mind is not a deliberately wanton force, replacing Providence, but, through chance as through other agencies, fate forces choices upon man; and man the actor must decide issues from within his bondage in circumstances. Thus Lohenstein reinterprets human finiteness rationally rather than religiously. Actual limitation is a well-spring of error; choice of any kind can be, as for Schiller's Wallenstein, the act of hubris which prompts tragedy. This holds especially when a decision must emerge from the victim's temporal position or comes within the field of his flaws. In the theater of history with its spectacles of doom, suffering is not the product of sin but of the natural condition; in this theater Lohenstein's characters parade in resistance to fate.

They play roles of extreme theatricality. And thus one task of the following chapters is to explain why fate and heroism are necessary corollaries in this reputedly unethical drama. Some equation is especially needed in the cases of the two African queens, whose destinies are bound up with their countries'. Misapplication of moral criteria clouds the significance of Lohenstein's frenetic heroism, shading into anti-heroism. But we must acknowledge the negativism that overwhelmed his drama, probably because he did not really share the new faith in the world process itself, when mechanistic philosophy reduced God to a proposition posited only to explain a system from which He had withdrawn after a perfectly successful act of creation. Lohenstein still portrays the jungle nature of the seventeenth century and explores the metaphor of the theater with psychologistic brooding, eschewing traditional religious explanation for the drama of arcane authorship. His work represents a shift in emphasis under the influence of ancient tragedy, which offered seventeenth-century playwrights a comparison; it explained hubris and nemesis through conditioning mythological stories in which tragic victims are enmeshed and whose skein reaches back into the tenebrous past, fading at last into the realm of fate. Long before Schiller or Hebbel, Lohenstein transfers tragic factors beyond human control from a religious basis to a historical basis, places the individual into actual, though still exemplary, historical situations, and centers interest upon the question of his freedom. In Gryphius spiritual freedom is at stake; in Lohenstein it is the whole range of freedom, from political liberty to inner independence. If any single thread runs through the whole dramatic fabric, it is the obsession with ever threatening bondage, which ultimately derives from the degrading transitoriness of man in his given role and from the laws of the world process. Lohenstein's origins are in the Gryphian ethos, as in *Ibrahim Bassa*, but he achieves an independent vision best represented in *Cleopatra* and *Sophonisbe;* in depicting the struggle to hold or gain freedom, he excludes neither the brutal fight of warrior nobles for unfettered existence nor the inner triumph in the quest of ideals.

Lohenstein is certainly of lower aesthetic stature than the poet Gryphius, who created an often beautiful dramatic idiom; Lohenstein's manneristic, exaggerated flux of speech does not compare. And yet, by secularizing the central concern for man's freedom, Lohenstein is a worthy successor. This achievement needs exploration. Critics have isolated most of the important dualities, such as Just's "energies," but the paramount European urge for freedom has not been recognized as the impulse in a polarity with degrading forces loosed by fate. We must, however, not fall into the old error of assigning a moralizing label to "freedom," simply in order to have a "value." Former criticism has wanted to see dualities like "reason-passion" as equivalent to "positive-negative." But Lohenstein's fascination with passion, and likewise with the ambiguous status of reason as a tool in cynical power struggle, belies such a convenient judgment. The propositions are not always distinct or concentrated all in one play. Nevertheless, the playwright attempts to show two things: like Gryphius, the conflict between man's finite limitations and infinite aspirations; unlike Gryphius, an impersonal, arcane, and incommensurable nemesis inherent in the world. This inevitability which opposes man and turns his strivings into a kind of hubris does indeed suggest the *Vanitas* motif of the seventeenth century. But ignoring the Christian hope for redemption, Lohenstein reopens the ancient wound of the universe which the sacrifice on the Cross promised to heal and which theodicy tried to explain away. By having "no such strength of religion and character," Lohenstein gives in to hideous doubts about the unfolding script of the great drama; his uncertainties represent a significant early groping for a modern tragic formula in German.

Chapter Two

THE MARTYRDOM OF RATIONAL AND
SENTIMENTAL IDEALISM

THE SEVENTEENTH CENTURY brought forth many tales of passion and intrigue in the exotic Orient, which actually extended far onto the European Continent with the Turkish empire. The sultan's absolutism, the intimate connection of religion and state, and the militant spirit of the Turkish nobles were impressive subjects; the Orient also offered convenient foreign dress in which to parade the manners of one's own age. Doubtless the very real threat presented by this foreign despotism suggested to Lohenstein, as to numerous authors, the setting for a representative drama of Europe's own internal struggle between the forces of tyranny and liberty. Using terms of contemporary philosophy and psychology, he certainly drew a clear line between safe and dangerous ground. The Turkish pieces have, therefore, a double function: to show the conflict between that which is ideally "European," i.e., victorious reason, and that which is "Oriental," i.e. the enslaving passions; and to examine the confrontation between sheer political power and individual conscience.

Lohenstein's orientation to the Turkish materials, borrowed from the Novel *Ibrahim ou l'illustre Bassa* by Mlle de Scudéry in von Zesen's translation (1645), was from the beginning both ethical and historical. He wished to expose "Turkish" greatness as deceptive. In a prologue Asia appears chained to figures representing the vices and bewails her lot under the Ottoman yoke. She portrays herself as fallen, tormented by inward corruption, a mask of outward splendor. An entire civilization, which gave religions and empires to the world, is passing away forever. She sees herself as an actress upon a world stage, "the theater of this earth," and helplessly caught in her role of decline (*I. B.*, I, 59–60). Doom, corruption, and lack of freedom are connected (I, 65).

Thus the dramatic action plays against a backdrop of timeless and manifest values. When the vacillating sultan threatens the lovers Ibrahim and Isabelle, we are to remember that a final court, the tribunal of history, sits in judgment over his reign. Soliman's rule is but a chapter in the sickness and decay of an empire. Isabelle's final speech, really an epilogue, carries a specific message for the times. She wants to tell the world her story and thereby excite it into a crusade against the miscreant civilization which has wronged her. This tendentious, propagandistic aim fits the pattern of martyr plays like Gryphius' *Catharina von Georgien* (1647). When the Shah of Persia, Catharina's passionate captor, threatens the queen, who will not marry him and violate religious scruples, her martyrdom provokes Christian sympathizers to holy war. Lohenstein likewise excites edifying sadness and a sense of outrage for noble sufferers. He makes clear that, in spite of Ibrahim's unjust execution and Isabelle's bereavement, these lovers triumph spiritually over the sultan. Yet their triumph does not occur, as does Catharina's victory, through or because of religion alone when, like her, they refuse to alter their individual resolutions or to gainsay their reciprocal oaths. With the fortitude of martyrs they resist absolute power and its total threat to their being; their loyalty contrasts with Soliman's wavering, betrayal, and duplicity; unshakable certainty lifts them above his miserable inner emptiness and doubts. But their appeal to a higher instance of judgment, to a legality over the demands of their ruler, does not express dogmatic faith.

Although pale rebels in the Gryphian tradition, Ibrahim and Isabelle do not stand on religious rights but rather on absolute rights of the human being. For they take refuge in a claim of personal freedom from all earthly coercion on behalf of an immediately experienced, terrestrial happiness, their marriage. It is by asserting this authority to which they are sworn that they rise above all vicissitudes; their ethical behavior is founded on secular, amorous fidelity, and their love vow, springing from inward choice, represents freedom of conscience. Thus love becomes the protagonist in its own right against the antagonistic forces which, as in Gryphius' plays, operate to undermine spiritual liberty. The dichotomy of love and politics is evident in *Ibrahim Bassa* in two parties, one consisting of intriguers who seek to manipulate the sultan and who poison his mind against the couple, the other made up of the threatened pair and an honorable courtier, Achmat, who wants to exert a better influence.[23] Both at the personal and at the state level, the conflict centers around a struggle against enslavement. The play begins with the situation of captivity; Ibrahim has failed in his flight toward Christian territory to protect his spouse and to find happiness in asylum beyond the rancor of the court. Enraged by this attempted escape from his control, which he would exercise even upon the private lives of his subjects, Soliman also fears deception. He is too weak to cope with scheming and thus is easily convinced that his best general, Ibrahim, has perhaps betrayed him to Christian plotters. No longer factually a Christian, Ibrahim regrets only defamation of his character and reviews his services to the realm in complete faithfulness. He insists that his flight was a personal, not a political, action. His desperation may not be stated distinctly in terms like those later used by Rousseau, but disgust with the social and political world is evident. That yearning, so powerful in the seventeenth century, the Christian desire to transcend earthly bondage, has secular application in the rejection of the prince's court, the center of society and, therefore, of corruption.

When Ibrahim must enter the dungeon under sentence of death, Isabelle inveighs not against the physical cruelty but the heartless separation of lovers. She longs to die, too, and sees delay of death as a harsh deprivation. The play does not raise a religious issue for martyrdom, but a proud and ecstatic thirst for suffering fills the heroine, who wants to face extinction "like a Christian" (*I. B.*, I, 365–68). In Isabelle, to die like a Christian is a nihilistic wish, yet also a desire for ultimate proof of, and permanence in, her love. The lovers aspire to consummate their union with a supreme homage, to give up life, where happiness would otherwise normally be possible, on behalf of their belief in such happiness. Their first parting resembles an operatic duet upon fated love. Though the tyrant causes the actual suffering, they cannot help but realize that they are choosing inevitable doom. No guilt is attached to such love so far elevated over base passion. But the heart, by insisting on its own triumph, brings about a noble downfall. The heart, then, on the verge of Racine's sphere, becomes the force working a tragic destiny. Thus Ibrahim cries out that he is cursed because he loves, that is, because his love may destroy Isabelle (I, 393–95). Even if freely entered into, love plays the part as a fatal determiner, when it, too, puts forward an absolute claim. In proclaiming its impossible mandate, it parades heroically and stoically upon the world's stage (I, 402).

This noble bearing one expects in an edifying spectacle of Gryphian tone, in which aristocratic personages suffer in exemplary manner. Achmat, an internal and ideal spectator of the drama, interprets the events in the love story as "tragedy" (I, 405–6). He also connects the term with traditional themes of the prince who has been raised up and cast down by fortune's wheel. Ibrahim has exactly such a role as a plaything of fickle chance, being a captive slave who has risen through unforeseen opportunity to the highest post of vizier, only to be returned to the dungeon. Lohenstein is uniting two dramatic traditions, the play of martyrdom and the play about the fall of a prince, under the newer sentimental and secular banner of love. We are expected to respond equally to the lovers' sudden reversals of fortune, which the author carefully develops in succeeding acts, and to their hopeless commitment to something sublime, on whose behalf they are condemned to suffer.

The play's first chorus, the plaint of the enslaved Christians, reinforces the sense of the first act. Like the prologue of suffering Asia, it calls into the audience's mind the actual menace of the Turks. Also it expresses an attitude shared by the protagonists, that of prisoners longing for freedom and subjected to a constant overhanging death sentence. In the choral strophe, the captives doubt and fear, even questioning whether God watches their torment. The antistrophe replies by referring to God's total plan, in accordance with which all things, even their suffering and the afflicting evil, are ultimately explained. This chorus is a rare dramatic moment in Lohenstein because, despite all pessimism, it depends on the notion of theodicy. A divinely ordained, prefigured justice will someday lift the curse and redeem the bitter temporality in which they pine. Without recourse to such an answer, promised vindication of God's world, the prisoners' question would suggest a non-Christian and tragic view of history. In the acts of the play the lovers' faith in their union is the parallel belief which gives to sacrifice a reassuring meaning. Without an absolute assurance, not martyrdom, a triumph under the guise of defeat, but real tragedy, defeat by an unexplainable doom, would occur. Love, like the Christian faith of the chorus' prisoners, guarantees a spiritual nullification of inescapable death.

The epode, an agonized cry for lifting of Turkish slavery and for revenge, certainly appeals to the seventeenth-century audience, but it really emphasizes less the distant final victory of God than some direct deliverance from oppression. The captives' desire for the fall of the oppressor Turk has the same immediacy as the heroes' thirst for execution, that is, fulfilment of an ever looming death sentence, for release—and final justification. The *entr'acte* not only stirs audience resentment against the antihero, Soliman, but interprets the entire physical setting and situation of the drama. In order to maintain a sealed empire with absolute control, the sultan has intercepted the flight of his best statesman to the outside—to freedom, which Christendom territorially represents. Physically, Europe is the "beyond"; spiritually, it means emancipation. Although in bondage, the captives have the seed of this beyond in them, especially their memories of home; and despite his control of the outward or physical situation, Soliman cannot master this inwardness. The play deals, moreover, with two lovers who have come originally from the "beyond" into servitude and have sought to return in order to regain freedom, the necessary condition imposed by love. Now, although unable to escape Turkish chains except through death, the couple still profess their love, that seed of the beyond in them. This "unrealistic" adherence to love as a principle leads, as subsequent acts show, to death.

While we may accept the first chorus, or Christian rationalization of suffering, as a systematic view, this suggestion of theodicy scarcely clothes the glaring irrationality in the martyr-lovers. Lohenstein's youthful work seems to renew the outline of a religious myth of man, exiled and enslaved, seeking the way back to the state of paradise. But there is often a hysterical note of eagerness in his searchers, who are too ready to try the road of death, who are trying to prove their nobility by a grand gesture. Like the personification Asia, Isabelle is conscious of acting a role and appealing to a judgment somewhere beyond the footlights of a world-stage in her monologue opening the third act:

Schaut/urtheilt ob ein Mensch im Schau–Platz diser Erden
Durchs Himmels Hass und Neid mehr kan geängstigt wärden.

(III, 5–6)

Such stoic pride, however cast in a Christian mold, is revealing; one discovers in Isabelle the roots of all later Lohensteinian heroines who spite an obdurate heaven. Nevertheless, she sees a God who is somehow the higher enacter and judge of the drama in which she is caught:

GOtt/mächtigster Erretter
Printz aller Printzen Printz/lass uns dis Vnglüks–Wetter
Nicht gar in nichts verkehrn; wo nicht/hilf/das der Nacht
Des Kerkkers/uns der Tod geschwind ein Ende macht.

(III, 73–76)

The concept of fortune, "misfortune's storm," or inconstancy of the world, and the theme of captivity, "the dungeon's night," merge. Rather than surrender her constancy, her love, her role, Isabelle would escape. Later heroines go beyond her position and choose suicide. A Christian is not permitted, except in martyrdom, any solution for the darkness, duplicity, and debasement that directly afflict him. He has only his inner guide.

The first lines of the final act summarize grandly the tragic import of the play's themes. Naturally the sultan's enticements and threats shake neither of the lovers. The ideal of love keeps them constant in the midst of perfidy; human reason sheds light in the prison-house of the senses. But although the protagonists share an attitude rather than a passion, experience a reasoned sentiment rather than physical attraction, it does not follow that they can cope with the real world. The false security of a momentary reprieve blinds Ibrahim to the dangers of the sultan's baseness. His forthrightness or non-political position has generally exposed him to the machinations of the intrigue. In the fifth act his love seems to lead him irresistibly toward extinction. He sounds blissful, but his language of happiness is laden with masochistic images and expresses tremulous expectations. Ibrahim's fleeting minute of joy reverberates like a martyr's embrace of annihilation:

IE finsterer die Nacht/ie häller ist das Liecht;
Je öfter man die Hand an spitzge Dörner sticht

35

Ie mehr bekränzt man sich mit Blut-bemilchten Rosen. . . .
Der Trauer–Rauch hat sich verkehrt in sanfte Wonne;
Die Nacht hat sich verhellt in eine lichte Sonne.

(V, 1–3, 11–12)

Ibrahim's love feeds on suffering and glows brighter with greater darkness. Implied in the force of love, even here in its most positive manifestation, is the property of ecstatic *blindness*. Before the final sentencing, Isabelle looks forward to a joint martyrdom. While her nobility prompts an in part permissible urge for death, her readiness for sacrifice verges on secular suicide and her words foreshadow the purely pagan love-death of Anthony in *Cleopatra*:

Es ist ja Trost/nicht Pein/
Wenn zwei/die nur ein Hertz/zwar in zwei Leibern leben/
Zusammen Seel und Geist und träue Lib aufgeben.

(I. B., V, 98–100)

The lovers do not, of course, overstep the limits of martyrdom—passive suffering for principles—even though they provoke Soliman to act as the murderous instrument. After so much passive suffering, the play's final call to action vents the pent-up anger implicit in the plot. But a characteristic *irrational* impulse, constantly tugging, is never allowed to disrupt the rather too sublime solution through Virtue and Reason.

Let it be said once again, to avoid the confusion which results from the history of the word "reason" after the seventeenth century, that a twentieth-century reader steeped in psychological studies must suspect these heroes' "Reason" when it leads them to equate freedom and death.

When, after Ibrahim's execution, Achmat bears tidings to Isabelle that she and the Christian prisoners may go home to their fatherlands, it is evident she feels disgust for earthly things. Freedom, literal freedom, no longer means anything to her; it only suffices, without Ibrahim, as a symbol of inner freedom. Death has become the central issue of life, and Isabelle lives on only on behalf of a meaning in Ibrahim's sacrifice, to proclaim their story to the world. With sentimental regret that she could not die with her beloved (V, 276–80), Isabelle morbidly apostrophizes his severed head. Such gruesome devotion points the way toward Lohenstein's later and more grisly "theatricality" of death. Isabelle clutches the head like a sacred relic. She is elevated to the stature of an evangelist, not so much of a religious faith, but rather of a historical mission, to lead a sacred war of "Freedom," to bring about the collapse of the Turkish empire, the symbolic and contemporary realm of tyranny, the dark inconstant land of passion. The ideal of freedom, originally presented incarnate in the private claim to happiness by the lovers, now ascends as representative of a noble urge into the political arena. Because the sentimental story of fated love acquires significance against the background of passion and slavery, love becomes finally a contrasting phenomenon with repercussions on a world scale. This fact should be emphasized. The political overtones in the suit of love is unmistakable. Early in *Ibrahim Bassa*, Isabelle puts a key challenge to Soliman: "If the emperor loves us, then let him set us free." ("Libt uns der Keiser denn so mach Er uns doch frei" [III, 124].) Love as the heroine knows it, as a state of freedom, is diametrically opposed to love as the tyrant experiences it, a blind captivity by unhemmed passions.

Although the issue may still be entangled with seventeenth-century concerns about freedom per se under the human condition, the issue is there, long before Schiller *(Kabale und Liebe)* and others dealt with it. Love stands for primary, inalienable rights; love opposes tyranny and necessitates freedom; a return to the rule of love redeems mankind. This possibility of redemption, which actually does occur with the sultan's change of heart, puts Lohenstein's first play, *Ibrahim Bassa*, close to the revolutionary sentimentalism of the next century. The partial enlightenment of Soliman's divided, sick heart is a token triumph of those forces which later storm the citadel of courtly, absolutistic Europe. But Lohenstein never returns to this idealism again in his dramas, except to show it in isolation as one of many *factors* determining human existence; and thus even a radical heroine like Epicharis could not appeal to the future, because Lohenstein treated her as tragic *fact* but not the total answer.

In his play of the anti-hero, *Ibrahim Sultan*, Lohenstein returns twenty years later to the subject matter of the original Turkish drama: freedom of will versus helpless determination. The conflict is basically the same; in the second Turkish play, chaste love and virginity face the threat of tyrannical abuse. The action opens with Ibrahim's attempted rape of Sisigambis, widow of his murdered brother. Her pure devotion to the memory of her husband inflames the sultan; beauty awakens the ugly depths of animal nature. However, the idea of fated love, which sadly edifies in the first Turkish drama, assumes sinister meaning in the villain. For Ibrahim fate is merely an excuse, justification for his own surrender to unbridled lust (I, 49–50). And yet there is a note of unfortunate truth in his statement about this kind of "fate," for he impresses us as a man condemned to inner emptiness, a man provoked by the divine excitant of beauty and worth, as these are incarnated in the noble widow. This means, at the same time, a threat for the beautiful and worthy human being whose divine qualities attract the passions of the world.[24] Ibrahim Sultan makes a different absolute claim on behalf of what he calls "Love," asserting that no oath or law binds it and that, as a creation of nature, it overpowers reason (I, 126–30). Thus, by being inconstant, he breaches the immutable rule of greatness of soul, whereas Sisigambis, insisting upon her vow, fights to maintain an image of herself, to control her own role. This inner image and inherent nobility go together. Lohenstein links the question of conscience with a conflict between the individual's claim to personal liberty and the state's or ruler's intrusion upon it when Sisigambis protests: "No prince, no Ibrahim rules over consciences" (I, 151). Her attitude antedates that of the Marquis de Posa in the famous confrontation with King Philip in Schiller's *Don Carlos*. The opening, hectic scene of violence presages the destiny of Ambre, upon whom Ibrahim Sultan's attention next turns.

Ambre, the daughter of the Mufti, aspires to a spiritual life. To avoid the sultan's will, she binds herself by oath to remain a virgin until she has completed a pilgrimage. Ibrahim is finally so enraged that he violates her, and this wild desecration provokes the political crisis which unseats him, for the disgruntled leaders of Turkey see in Ambre their symbol of strength and value. Ambre's opening speech is a prayer already clothing her in the habit of a martyr. The central issue comes forth, that of reason versus the animal passions, of light versus darkness (II, 6). She swears to remain directed by her inner image of God and asks that the pure picture not be extinguished in her (II, 21). The relativity of Lohenstein's concern for the dogmatic religious issues is, however, evident; Ambre is actually a devout Mohammedan. More important is her consciousness, like Isabelle's, of the world-stage where one's life becomes a role or test, which one plays well or ill. History, very much in the Christian sense still, is a place of judgment, a "show-place" *(Schau–Platz)* where true souls are often deceptively distinguished by torments; of this, Ambre is already convinced (II, 31–37).

Ambre's ideal of permanence depends less on the sway of a transcendental godhead than on her yearning to comply with an indefinable agency, which she calls expressly "Fate"

(Verhängnis). The Christian deity is conspicuously absent as regulator and judge of the testing grounds of history, and history alone remains to evince the workings of the inscrutable power to which Ambre turns. Fame replaces immortality of the soul, but since the realm of fate is timeless, death is the sole gateway to permanence (II, 367–71). From her first moment on stage, her whole orientation is toward dying: "Who lives saintly already tastes heaven on earth" (II, 386). After being raped, she curses her own beauty, that fateful attractiveness incarnate in the flesh, and expresses loathing for her own body (IV, 140–44). But in connecting beauty with the image of the stars, Ambre reveals also that it belongs ambiguously to the province of destiny:

> Die Schönheit ist ein Stern/der mit dem Schwantz allzeit
> Auf neues Unheil weisst/ein Abgott/der entweiht
> Von derer Andacht wird/die sich zum Opfer finden/
> Weil sie für Weyrauch ihm meist stinckend Hartzt anzünden.
>
> (IV, 145–48)

The antithesis, "carrion" and "star," expresses the dual possibility for human beauty, which as flesh must suffer death but as spirit may win "immortality," fame. Thus, when Ambre kills herself in order to be remembered and avenged and her suicide provides a case against the sultan which a nucleus of his officers need in order to depose him, her combination of Roman virtue and of saintly removal is not just the passive role of a Christian martyr. By taking her own life, she does what no saint may do.

Although Isabelle is moved at the end of *Ibrahim Bassa* to act as crusader and Ambre commits suicide for revenge, their roles are the acting out of a progressively more pessimistic attitude of inner dignity. If Ibrahim and Isabelle have, at least briefly, a factual union, the love pact of the Begler–Beg of

Roumania and Ambre is without the slightest suggestion of the flesh. His courting is reverential and his affection spiritual. Amorously seen, he has the least color of all Lohenstein's males. In contrast, a frantic energy and unrest fills the women of the seraglio. In *Ibrahim Bassa,* for example, Roxelane joins forces with the most sinister courtier, Rusthan, and the Islamic church, in order to overthrow the bassa, not because the latter threatens her in fact, but because she fears his potential power. Similarly, she envisions Isabelle as somehow more devious and crafty than herself, a perfect deceiver to whom she may lose her own hard-won status. Practised in deception and beguilement, Roxelane has mastered the weapons of passion. She is a political woman, resolute as are the heroines, but calculating. To her the world seems a game, all appearances a mask which "reason and cunning and understanding" (IV, 51) must penetrate; she uses reason only as a practical tool. While Isabelle prefigures Ambre and the grimly determined Epicharis, Roxelane already suggests the frantic figure of Agrippina. But Roxelane's character does not yet pose any of the puzzling questions later raised about antiheroic behavior, because she does not appear to suffer and is still too much a sketch.

The terror of political man driven to anticipate and outcalculate the workings of history is more evident in the Ottoman queens in *Ibrahim Sultan* who are forced to intrigue for the sake of their own and their children's safety. Sekierpera, the procuress, eager to ingratiate herself with the sultan, cannot fail to endanger the already established wives. Nor can Kiosem, the queen mother, stand aside from scheming, lest a new and dangerous figure move closer to the ruler and perhaps turn him against her. She must be cruel and devious, and has already had poisoned, for example, the only woman whom he has ever really loved. Consequently, the sultan is a potential enemy among potential enemies, a prey to subterfuge and a victimizing counteractor. All tend to violate natural bonds and the holiest laws because of their political impulse. Through its very structure, the court spawns crime.

The two Turkish plays are inferior representatives of Lohenstein's drama, but they serve to illustrate his deepening negativism. The preciosity of noble love in *Ibrahim Bassa* gives way to the horrible specter of bestial madness in *Ibrahim Sultan;* the spotlight shifts from the hero to the antihero. When Lohenstein turns, in his Roman plays of 1665, from contemporary to ancient history, he frees himself somewhat from the restraints of his original orientation; nevertheless, the stage is still the corrupt court, the political world. In the Turkish plays, one indication that time is out of joint is, of course, the need for revenge against authority. In the Roman plays, corrupt earthly government cannot be altered; it merely reflects the sway of an iron law, a higher authority in the universe.

Chapter Three

THE MARTYRDOM OF POLITICAL IDEALISM

LOHENSTEIN's *Epicharis* and *Agrippina* appeared together in 1665, after Gryphius had published *Papinian* (1659). Twelve years separate the Roman dramas from *Ibrahim Bassa;* there is likewise a gap of twelve years between Gryphius' *Catharina von Georgien* and *Papinian*.[25] The pagan heroine Epicharis is better understood if contrasted with Gryphius' unambiguous, stern hero, the unbending lawyer whom Willi Flemming considers to be the supreme achievement of Germany's seventeenth-century theater, its noblest incorporation of "Ethos."[26] Although Papinian is her closest correspondent, the resemblance proves to be superficial; for he stands fixed and monumental, a frozen attitude, virtually a statue surrounded by numerous smaller copies, his family members who fill out the picture of virtue. They form a party inspired by one and the same principle; they die for this principle in one and the same manner, thus underscoring the hero's position. Rather than act deceitfully, inconstantly, or cowardly, he always affirms the truth, yet strives to maintain complete loyalty to Bassianus Caracalla, his prince. Caracalla has criminally and jealously slain his brother and clamors for justification, which only a respected moral authority, a Papinian, can pronounce. As antihero, the emperor represents the antiprinciple of a treacherous and inconstant world, man's political world. Papinian refuses to sanction the crime. But although he could easily overthrow Caracalla, in fact is begged to revolt by the army, he does not resist the vengeful sentence passed by the tyrant. The final act of the play develops to an operatic climax; it is a moving chorus of praise devoted not to any real action but to the hero's funeral.

43

Not Caracalla, but Papinian emerges as the triumphant figure. We must recognize him after the final proof of death as a great example, the stoic martyr overcoming for eternity an endangering world. He is buried before our eyes, removed into that timeless repository of great men and deeds called death.

Epicharis, too, commands the second half of the fifth act, in which her inner fortitude undergoes and emerges victorious from every test. A prisoner throughout most of the play, she plays the role of an unrelenting martyr, a passive sufferer under despotism. But she does more than merely affirm principle. The radical difference is that Epicharis also actively combats the antihero and never hesitates to betray her emperor. She starts as a crusader and claims the right to rebel, and it is a conspiratorial attempt which ensnares her in the chains of suffering. Whereas Papinian and Ibrahim Bassa remain obedient to an established order that has somehow become imperfect in its earthly expression, Epicharis refuses to accept worldly corruption as ordained, so absolute is her stand. She sees Nero as usurper of a divine order and his government as an instrument for evil. She strives to rally the remnants of the nobility in order to re-establish freedom, the original and heroic state of men under the Roman republic. In *Papinian* we witness the aftermath of man's fall, the time of tyrannic darkness in which solitary lights or examples passively remind us of higher principles; in *Epicharis* we witness a final struggle against the night.

The key fact is Epicharis' personal involvement with a varied collection of fellow conspirators in an abortive plot.[27] Although she distinguishes herself as the ideal figure among them, they, too, play a significant role in the formation and disintegration of a political party. This Lohenstein observes from a lofty height with silent impartiality, and for this "coolness," as negative critics put it, he is notorious. At times he can chill us with a brutality and cynicism which make us doubt his commitment to anything ideal.[28] But Lohenstein is deliberate rather than cynical in making his point: that Epicharis' whole inner being and aim are in contradiction to the historical development of Rome. Immediately after the crystallization of the plot, the soothsayer of the first chorus reveals the already written decree, "fate's decision" (I, 802). The personification "Fate" similarly interrupts and subordinates all speakers in the second chorus who argue about the determinative role of wits, chance, or the historical moment in human destiny; we learn that Fate's arcane power manifests itself through many complicated and intertwined agencies. In the third chorus, the Tiber and hills of Rome bewail the blood that flows and curse Nero's reign. They cannot bear the inflicted burden of fate, against which no scheming prevails. The Tiber wishes his waves could drown the tyrant; the hills pray for a catastrophic flood to cleanse themselves. Clearly Nero's position is alterable only by a change ordained in the order of things (III, 766–68).[29]

If, then, Epicharis presumes to contest against the decree of fate, how does her action affect the principle of freedom, which she advocates? The fourth chorus interprets her martyrdom by expounding Rome's significance in world politics. Europe, Asia, and Africa, the three continents comprising the Roman empire, complain bitterly of their enchainment to Rome and call to the gods for revenge. We shall also discuss this portrait of Rome as agent of fated enslavement in regard to the African plays. In *Epicharis*, Rome herself, the mother city, bewails her own sufferings at the hands of her own children, i.e., the Romans, and asks fate to take away her crown. The Cumaean Sibyl prophesies slavery and suffering for the Imperial City under tyrants. The enslaver, Rome, will be afflicted by what it has practised upon the world. Each ruler appears through an emblem; the first in an act of destruction: "Now a lion treads underfoot a golden form" (IV, 683). The vision is interpreted:

> Rom ist das Bild/die Freyheit war das Gold/
> Itzt aber ist in Eisen es gewandelt.
>
> (IV, 689–90)

Rome herself acknowledges that her rulers have mauled the great ideal of freedom:

> Wahr/leider ists. Des Caesars Löwen–Klauen
> Zermalmeten der Freyheit güldnes Bild.
>
> (IV, 695–96)

Epicharis struggles, therefore, on behalf of a hopeless cause; it is impossible to restore the lost nobility and past golden age, the original state from which the Romans have fallen. And freedom has become ambiguously a force leading her into conflict with fate and into perdition, since it is no longer obtainable through politics. No matter how earnestly desired, it lives on only internally, in man's spiritual life. Political man— so Lohenstein seems to say—is a tragic creature, if he strives for this ideal; he cannot regain his lost nobility through politics, because the mechanism of the state itself represents the antithesis of such freedom.

One senses at once in Epicharis' attitude the idealistic excess, the death-laden absolute demand, of a potential martyr. While the nobles of Rome chafe under Nero's tyranny and their own degradation, they look upon the loss of republican virtue and freedom as a fated process. To them Rome is irresistible, an organism destroying or absorbing both individuals and states. Epicharis, however, refuses to accept this idea of historical determinism and advocates man's freedom to choose his own path of conduct (I, 24–30). Making man responsible, she thereby restores to him the dignity of being more than a controlled creature; she views Nero as symptomatic of general moral degeneracy but not of necessary degeneracy. Attributing loss of nobility to guilty cowardice, she offers to die herself in demonstration of the inner worth she advocates, and can see only victory in such an enterprise; heroic honor, fame, is the reward (I, 85–89). When she invokes the nobles as "you heroes" (I, 89), her political program is literally to reconvert the Romans into a heroic race. Quite unlike a merely passive idealist, Epicharis wishes to impose her inner values by force, by manipulation, by politics upon an unheroic world. The discrepancy is, of course, that the world is unheroic because of something inherently evil in "politics," the corrupt instruments of deceit and coercion.

How differently Seneca talks in his first appearance. When Natalis interviews him in hope of winning his support, Seneca disputes that there is any legal justification for regicide. His position admits of no duplicity or crime, even in the name of justice. He acknowledges the absolute rule of his prince, accepts the evils of government as heaven's mandate and a natural curse, and refuses to sully himself with blood. His stoic resignation stands in the direct tradition of *Papinian,* passive compliance with destiny: "A wise man bears stout-heartedly what fate ordains" (I, 573). In contrast to Epicharis with her activist program, Seneca believes that the heroic sphere is inward and personal; one cannot impose one's own moral bravery upon the outward, temporal, and political arena of existence. Therefore he takes refuge in metaphysical truth, with complete neutrality toward the events in a turbulent world: "I shall not stand by you, also not by Nero" (I, 596). In precarious isolation between the opponents, his heart nevertheless speaks for the plotters and gives advice, in which sounds a fateful note: "My wish is your victory, my teaching: delay not" (I, 602). Lohenstein presents two figures, Seneca and Epicharis, so that a clear picture may emerge of man's total helplessness against destiny. On the one hand, Epicharis tries to shape destiny through sheer will; on the other hand, Seneca accepts fate. But regardless of their divergent attitudes, both are equally marked by doom.

The political idealist's mistake is to trust that he can control, can outwit, can outcalculate, the vast process in which he himself is only a single element. As soon as Epicharis presumes to use other individuals as instruments of her will and no longer views them as self-determined agents, she goes against the very principle she champions. The debate about Piso underlines the difficulty. Although many conspirators harbor misgivings that he only covets Nero's power, they regard him as their candidate, since they believe a dictatorship is the sole solution to Rome's problems. Epicharis foresees only more terrible corruption and tyranny if Piso is inwardly ignoble and sinful; they must establish true freedom or be doomed. The group compromises, agreeing to kill Piso after the rebellion and to replace him with Seneca, the one honorable figure, whom Epicharis proposes. To achieve her pure aim, she agrees to regicide and perfidious murder of a dupe; also, and thus Lohenstein shows the hopelessness of her political involvement, she selects as a necessary compromise to use the very two men who cannot or will not act. Epicharis, as but one member of a configuration of individuals, demonstrates one reality, human nobility and self-abnegation. Piso demonstrates another, cowardly opportunism. Seneca offers yet a third with his wisdom, resignation, and interest in his fame. The first act brings together a historical group whose collective story must be determined by the complicated entanglement of natures, motives, and attachments. These personalities Lohenstein treats carefully, no matter how small their part, in his effort to exhibit the great range of humanity and to show why, therefore, collectively mankind is enslaved. Because Lohenstein regards the whole, he can impress us as scientific and cold. But it is in his total vision, however pessimistic, that an Epicharis exists with unimpeached validity. She will not accept the facts of the human condition in general;

she rebels primarily against inherent baseness. Her hubris is the wish to make man more than he is in the world's established order, to free him from natural bondage, and to infuse in him a divine spirit. In addition, the human condition imposes limitations on her; even a hero is only half godlike. Epicharis cannot predict, as she presumes to do, the collective story in which she has a circumscribed, personal role. The unexpected and incalculable happens. Despite her prudish removal from love, Epicharis must now experience the threat of an external passion in Proculus, to whom she has mistakenly turned for help. Like Ambre, she has unwittingly atttracted worldly desires upon herself, and, through Proculus, fate protrudes menacingly into her existence.[30] A dark nimbus begins to descend. Scevin, concerned by the gravity of the undertaking to which he is sworn, tries to bolster his courage and prepare himself for the eventuality of death. His strange behavior, in freeing slaves, preparing a great feast at his house, drawing up his testament, and so forth, makes his freedman, Milichius, suspicious. Another passion, greed, prompts this servant and his wife to guess what is afoot and to betray him. Once more fate intrudes via the passionate and weak nature of man. Lohenstein is merciless in the exposition of the consequences. A reversal occurs for the role and value of veracity. The servants' fabricated story, a guess colored by them to gain more credence with the emperor, succeeds as a lie, because it imitates the truth. The evil figure, Nero, plays fact-finder; he ferrets out actuality by every kind of trick, but not on behalf of any pure "truth." Deceit must work for the nobles if they are to win against the epitome of treachery. But only Epicharis, the "pure" heroine, shows ability with her lies. The theme of duplicity staggers to newer heights as the political inquisition develops through acts three, four, and five. Ripping off veils of innocence in a terrified wave of panic and betrayal, the plotters strip confederates of their disguises, too. Thus an entire political movement unmasks itself—as weak,

maladroit, cowardly, sometimes pitifully base, yet also sometimes firm and admirable. High officers and respected soldiers,
when confronted by ignominious death, expose hidden moral
scars, unexpected flaws, very human debilities. As the mask
rises from the assembly, we see the gradation of humanity.
Here is a spectacle of *desengaño* on the grand scale of a
world theater.[31]

After the first act, nothing happens except a step by step
collapse of hope in this drama of political nemesis. The drama's
further subject is Epicharis' martyrdom against the background
of a political purge. The whirlpool draws in the name of
Seneca, too. He acknowledges that the noble stoic and the
political idealist have an inner affinity when he says: "She and
a wise man can feel the least pains" (V, 8). Both depend on
absolute faith. No earthly consideration can move Seneca, least
of all fear of ruination and death, because he takes refuge in
a divine and unassailable realm of freedom, his own spirit:

> Ja/wie die Götter selbst nichts schmertzliches empfinden/
> Wenn man ihr Bild zerbricht/die Tempel äschert ein:
> So/weil die Weisen ja auf Erden Götter seyn
> Und Geister über Sonn und Sternen in sich nehren/
> Kan Unfall zwar den Leib ihr blosses Bild verzehren/
> Nichts aber Irrdisches dem Geiste Schaden thun.
> Weil in nicht ausser ihm so Schatz als Wesen ruhn.
>
> (V, 56–62)

As in Epicharis' mind, such death means both release from and
victory over earthly bondage; in death is glory (V, 96–98).
Lohenstein, a fervent admirer, presents strong arguments to
absolve Seneca from any blame in connection with Nero's
monstrous development. The sage defends his own conduct
throughout life, despite all appearances or slander to the con-

trary, and rests upon the absolute security of his character as an inner truth: "With us matters what we are, not what one thinks of us" (V, 126). Despite anticourtly and antisocial invective, Seneca's attitude is pre-Rousseauian, tied with the Christian notion of blessed isolation, of saintly hermitage away from the madness of the world. In not resisting the external assault of tyranny, Seneca believes that he is obeying a dictate of fate (V, 235–37) and acting out at last the philosophy of which his works speak, centered around the correct attitude toward death (V, 243–46).

The act of dying is itself given an ironic twist. No matter how disgusted with life, Seneca must struggle physically to kill himself. This further test finally fills us with awe for the philosopher sardonic toward his own strength, the signs of life as it were in a protesting body (V, 304–5). Of course, Lohenstein exploits the historical details of the scene, the slashing of limbs, the taking of poison, and finally the hot bath to force the end—all of which was a favorite subject in the seventeenth century; the lugubrious and majestic triumph can still be appreciated with full emotional color through the music of Claudio Monteverdi's (1567–1643) opera *L'Incoronazione di Poppea*. Lohenstein utilizes the same technique in his scenes of torture and execution, achieving by repetition of critical moments a staggering of our emotions, and in this play draws closer than in any other to the Corneillean goal of exciting admiration rather than compassion. Epicharis' martyrdom sets the outermost limits, however, in goriness and horror.[32] Lohenstein has merely prepared us to sense deeper wonder before her spectacle. She shares Seneca's grim humor and infuses his spirit into some of the captives who are mutilated and slaughtered in front of her. Poppaea, Tigillinus, and Nero have entered the dungeon through compulsive need to triumph over the defiant girl, who frustrates them until they become rabid and commit atrocities before her only to break her mind.

She understands that their need to extinguish every light of liberty has driven them berserk (V, 698). Just before killing herself, Epicharis depicts the blackness and terror of Nero's soul, haunted by the ghosts of his victims, and speaks with axiomatic terseness of that polarity in humanity which her drama, and Nero's, has demonstrated: "Nero will live only through shame, I through virtue" (V, 732). She makes this final pronouncement as if reconciled with destiny and speaking with its authority. The secular orientation of Epicharis' goal, her distinctly earthly objectives of a political program, in no way exclude her from the highest province. She approaches that sphere by her heroism and enters it just as a Greek hero might through profound experience of his humanity and of doom. The re-establishment of a terrestrial Republic of Rome is a hopeless task, in fact equal to a religious mission to redeem men from corruption. Epicharis' aspiration is inspired, fanatic; in her heroics she similarly exceeds the boundaries of the normal and possible, enduring in an unnatural and virtually supernatural fashion; she rises above the common denominator of the weak flesh to assume a special rank, like a saint, but also like a Hercules, the model for travails, to whom she has masochistically referred (IV, 53–57).

Her final clarity of mind transfigures her. But Epicharis, who, like the ancient heroes, long seems indestructible even in body, succumbs at last to the most degrading extinction in surroundings of intense misery. All the while that her heart beats on for her cause, we witness the horrible spectacle of mutilation and inevitable death. This heroic pathway is the road of "blind" sainthood, a holiness outside the precincts of Christian dogmatic mission, elevation of a human being simply through pain. Epicharis refuses to give in to the facts of life and of man the creature; she struggles naïvely and unseeingly, so it seems, for a remote ideal. Yet her nature permits her sight of what is eternal and timeless. The picture of pure, noble, free man—a picture so bright and real before her eyes, but hidden largely from others—drives her forward. What is blindness in Epicharis from the point of view of normal humanity is holy vision from the point of view of higher humanity. The usual stern Roman stoic, whether Gryphius' Papinian or Lohenstein's Seneca, is, however, less pitiful, because he purposely withdraws from the hopeless entanglements of the world. Epicharis is compelled to resist futilely the onslaught of destiny.

In summary it can be said that the great attractiveness of Epicharis is her blind dedication, so different in the long run from mere stoic pessimism. While she becomes great through sheer suffering, it would, of course, be nonsense to claim that her motives are not ethical. In fact, just as Gryphius' Papinian is pathetic in gesture, so is Epicharis ethical in purpose. Although the majority opinion has held that Lohenstein is not "ethical" and therefore not a tragedian, the view is strangely inconsistent. If the play *Epicharis* approaches convincing tragedy, but does not achieve it, it is because the heroine is so steeped in ethical surety as to make herself impervious, i.e., "superhuman." In twentieth-century terms, she is "exaggerated," and, as a consequence, not pitiful or tragic. If we think in the Corneilleian terms, but from our present-day viewpoint, positive qualities outweigh to the extent that one speaks more of a play exciting admiration rather than compassion. But the roots of tragic pity could potentially draw nourishment from this soil. There is no wise retirement from the dangerous world; there is overconfidence in personal ability to oppose it. Such presumption is an ingredient in the hubris of the three sinful queens, Agrippina, Sophonisbe, and Cleopatra.

Chapter Four

CRIME AND DOOM

THE POLITICAL DRAMA *Epicharis* is also the story of the heroine's personal fate within and against the background of Roman historical development, which serves to explain her doom; she opposes with blind hope a universal, invincible process of enslavement. As in Greek drama, a prophecy has to be fulfilled, and a mysterious, impersonal decree requires the fall of the blindly struggling protagonist. For the Greeks a curse or oracle could affect the entire history of a family, so that causes and relationships finally stretched into mythological obscurity, far beyond the victim's control in the particular play in which one witnessed the tragic results of foregone doom. Lohenstein creates a substitute for the ancient *context*. The choruses in *Epicharis* give the "fore–" and "afterplay," or "fable," reveal truths beyond the temporal sphere of the play, here, of course, quite real historical circumstances beyond the heroine's control. Lohenstein, depending on his audience's knowledge of the infamous Neronian chapter and other facts of history, reworks them as a kind of mythological web in which the individual story is entangled. From the point of view of an audience in any historical period, all that has already happened stands fixed, immutable, and seems to have been "inevitable." This is the psychological basis of conviction also that contemporary and future events may be prefigured or determined. Lohenstein consciously draws together historicity and fate in *Epicharis*; and by using historical subject matter as the equivalent of mythological tradition, he creates the equivalent of a drama of nemesis.

55

The play *Agrippina* also is embedded in a context. The choruses reveal to the audience the close connection between moral issues and political development for Rome. In the first choral interlude, a disputation, the question arises why men cannot see the light of reason, which is directly equated with virtue, and whether vice or virtue affords man genuine satisfaction. Virtue, however, is evidently regarded as a heroic attitude against the world rather than a pious activity aimed at supernatural reward, and brings in itself its own reward. And the Christian principle of justice continues only as a hollow shell, for the disputation makes it clear that retribution can only occur in history or through the witness of history, in so far as man suffers from bad conscience while alive or fears a bad reputation when dead (I, 668–70). With no eternity of hell or heaven for the soul, with only the possibility of securing a good or a bad memorial, we can comprehend why virtue must indeed strike a stoic pose. Immortality has become monumentality. The deeper level of this disputation, its emotional bias, is a concluding metaphor reminiscent of *Epicharis*, IV, 57, or of *Ibrahim Sultan*, II, 6:

> Denn: Dass ihr ja der Tugend Nectar schmeckt/
> Eh als ihr solt verfinstert leben/
> Muss ein Tyrann ans Licht euch heben.
>
> (I, 678–80)

The tyrant, as the agent of darkness, plays a role similar to the theological function of the devil, providing the challenge and threat of evil and an exemplary contrast. This justification of the tragic principle is general.

The second chorus is the specific example of a pure martyr, the Vestal virgin Rubria, whom Nero has defiled. The Vestals comment like a Greek classic chorus on the happenings of the drama and connect the events in Rome with traditions concerning the city's foundation and prognosticated fall. The legend is that Aeneas brought with him from Troy the holy fire and an image of Pallas, the goddess traditionally connected with reason. As long as the image survived, the city was to live. Of course, the Vestals themselves carefully tended the temple of the sacred fire. It symbolized by its continuance the perseverance of the home of the Romans; a dead fire meant the extinction of civic life, the reduction to ashes of their existence. (Vesta, goddess of both the public and private hearth, chose to be an old maid; Lohenstein, therefore, associates her with the virgin deity of reason, whose image the Vestals simultaneously perpetuated.) Now the virgins lament bad omens for the image and fire, and Rubria interprets these by referring to the story of Helen and the fall of Troy:

> So bald in Ilium der Geilheit Brunst entglam/
> Und Paris Helenen dem Menelaus nam;
> Ward unser Feuer auch verzehrt.
> So bald ihr Tempel ward befleckt
> Entwiech die Göttin weg/ihr Bild ward fortgetragen;
> Gantz Troja ward in Brand gesteckt.
>
> (II, 508–13)

This authoritative myth reveals the ambiguous significance of the fire; it has borne a curse since remote time. On the one hand, it represents the life force of a people, and its loss or transfer means the termination of empire. On the other hand, through defilement, this life force breaks out wildly and consumes its housing, whether temple, city, or nation. The unruly passions devastate both men and states, and contagious vice signals collapse—historical doom. This is an ever popular theory.

In European literature of the seventeenth century, however, fire and flame are standardized metaphors for love or passion. Lohenstein now widens the scope of these fixed emblems to

57

include also all destructive forces, whether national corruption or personal weaknesses. He creates thereby a prefigurative mythology of the imperial family; for the house of the Caesars, he emphasizes, descends from Aeneas *and* Venus. Aeneas brought holy fire, the life force, in order to establish Rome; Venus gave the passions, flames of love, which would later put the Roman state into conflagration. Pallas, the chaste and rational deity whose image protects the city, will remove to another people. This other folk, hinted at in this chorus of *Agrippina* as inheritors of the empire, is distinguished through a promise of eternal reign, should it remain pure.[33] Rubria accuses Nero as the dangerous new Paris who defiles the sancti-ties and starts the destructive blaze which must waste Rome:

> Ich seh in Rom schon Trojens Brand/
> Von Agrippinen ist die Fackel ja gebohren;
> Dem Otho wird Poppe' entwand/
> Und für die Helena das Käyserthum verlohren.

> (II, 527–30)

Thus the play's heroine no longer fits in the ranks of the martyrs Isabelle, Ambre, or Epicharis, for she herself has given new issue to the curse of political and social doom, in her son Nero. Agrippina belongs rather with those ancient tragic figures who carry within themselves the seeds of destiny. Lohenstein carefully points out that on every level, political, moral, and even biological, Fate emerges upon the curse-bearing queen. She has given birth to her own murderer and to a monstrous tyrant. The playwright literally provokes the audience in its historically grounded expectations, when Rubria prophesies ecstatically that a son will kill his lascivious mother, and later be wet with his own blood (II, 559–62).

In Nero we see twinned excesses of politics and love, the duality (Aeneas–Venus) which the choruses treat. The opening

scene of the first act reveals the tyrant prating about his absoluteness and Rome's golden age under his scepter, all of which
should make him the most fortunate of mortals. But his extreme
claim, his thirst for immortality betray the opposite of what he
intends. The initial words, "So ist's" (I, 1) describe, ironically
as the audience is soon aware, a moment of corrupt power;
Nero has no control over the course of events but, caught up
in political and erotic currents, is, rather, representative of a
phase of history.[34] Nero overweeningly vaunts that his image
will stand "in the temple of true souls" (I, 27). Because of
inner insecurity, he makes exaggerated demands upon the world
outside him for recognition. Nero's political power allows him
to mistake his own whims for law and leads him into the
danger of self-alienation, a transfer of his self out upon the
surrounding world.[35] He is actually incapacitated for knowing
his own "will" in the higher sense, and this is the direst situation for the seventeenth century, whose slogan is *gnothi se*.
Otho's scheming boast that Poppaea's beauty makes him feel
like a *god* achieves the desired result, for Nero, the would-be
god, sighs loudly and exposes his scarred heart (I, 144) which
smarts beneath pompous royal pretenses. Absolute in political
power, but a vessel of torments and prey to infatuations, in
him the drives of rulership and of eroticism intertwine dangerously. Lohenstein just antedates Racine, who also presents
a dangerous Nero, hopelessly jealous and unstable, tragically
manipulated by an alter ego, Narcisse, in *Britannicus* (1669).

The second scene expands our vision of Nero, who would
lash out at once against a suspected threat by his mother
Agrippina. It is of little importance whether her accusers tell
the truth or not in this court atmosphere of deceit and anxiety.
What matters is that their report *could* be veracious, since she
has every reason to be plotting against her son, who has stripped
her of her former political power and, as we learn, has also
made clumsy attempts upon her life. Nero betrays the forlorn

uncertainty of political man, for whom all bonds of loyalty, all sure foundations of truth, have crumbled, even the elemental ties of nature in the family (I, 248). Nero's actual isolation is as extreme as his claims of greatness, since even this limited moral sphere of nature becomes a jungle through politics. And from the onset Agrippina plays the role of a caged animal desiring freedom. She exaggerates house arrest into imprisonment (I, 284). Hurt by the abeyance of her renown, based on her former political power, she feels "more than forgotten" (I, 287) and, therefore, assumes the pathetic pose of a fallen noble, a shipwrecked example of the world's treacherous changes (I, 291, 294). Lohenstein ironically and carefully announces through her rhetoric the dominant themes of her endangerment, the first faint intimations of doom. In the fourth act Agrippina experiences not a rhetorical but an actual treacherous shipwreck! Octavia sees Nero as a violent and debauched husband, whom her own wifely virtue repulses, while Agrippina sees further that he is potentially murderous (I, 351–52). Thus her urge to return to court and denounce Octavia's and her own calumniators is motivated finally by sheer necessity.

Agrippina's majestic attributes represent the fundamental danger to her tyrannical son. He wants literally to be deified, but she asserts: "I did not make myself a servant, nor him an idol" (I, 370). This noble claim connects her with the heroes of freedom, the stoic and political martyrs. Her resoluteness in the face of danger also makes that clear. She uses practically the same words as Ibrahim Bassa (*I. B.*, I, 217) in scorning the threat of death (*Ag*, I, 415), and, like Epicharis, continues only by dint of will power. Although Agrippina realizes that the lawful relationships of the family are dead (I, 433) and finds herself caught in the same unnatural, political net as her son, she does not rebel heroically against this world; rather, she works entirely within the Roman court and state, vainly seeking to manipulate them. She thinks that she is clever when, to stir pity, she refers to her case as a tragic spectacle: "This is the tragedy which already is beginning with me." ("Diss ist das Trauerspiel/das schon mit mir beginnet" [I, 439].) In making this statement, Agrippina both knows and does not know its full import. Because of her ever vital hope, she argues with conscious pretense of theatricality; because of her fear, she unwittingly pronounces the truth. She speaks, therefore, in the strange manner of the doomed, by her own mouth, the chilling oracle which Fate ironically releases. Thus she is no longer really a martyr type as much as a presumptuous victim. Her role, more-over, fits the seventeenth-century genre of the "actor of himself," drama in which a character believes he acts in a role or in pretense, but grows progressively more captive in and ultimately *becomes* the role undertaken; the "play" is unmasked as reality.[36] Of course, in Lohenstein's age when theater itself is the great metaphor of existence, self-consciousness is expressed as aware-ness of being an actor, and one's role is the most important experience.[37] In the role of the unknowingly blind victim, the queen enjoys a false victory through her powers as an actress— she achieves a reconciliation. Playing desperately for life and honor on the real stage of the world, she must seize the extreme means to excite remorse, and thus renounces her motherhood, while also emphasizing her motherly readiness to shed her blood. Her pathos seems all the more ominous through its radical success. Nero changes so far in his passing phase of regret that he sets in office Agrippina's favorites and banishes her enemies; such rashness can only portend another more drastic reversal of her fortune, for it shows once more his personal weakness. Nero's clutching for childlike security also emphasizes how radical the break in morally "natural" relation-ships has been and may again be. The second act shows Poppaea's rapid rise to power, extinguishing Agrippina's gain. For sake of comparison, one can listen to the now ecstatic, now morose, tones in Monteverdi's *Incoronazione di Poppea*. This opera, as mentioned, treats the stoic greatness of Seneca's suicide, the banishment of the royal women through the adventuress' ascent, and also the cruel, ruthless passion of a mating that recognizes no laws other than desire and wilfulness. In *Agrippina* love is treated amorally as a natural force to be tapped for power. Seneca and Burrhus criticize Octavia for her purity, for not competing sexually with her rivals, and, sensing the shift in fortune, decide not to resist the emperor. The system of monogamy and chastity is cynically evaluated as meaningless. As in the court of Louis XIV, erotic amorality and erotic power characterise feminine politicking.

To stand upon one's purity, innocence, or nobility, without participating in politics, virtually means choosing extinction.[38] Agrippina knows that removal from the court means potential death (II, 435). She has very little choice but to give in to the promptings of the jungle law and use her erotic powers, even though thereby she transgresses that other moral "nature," the taboo of family relationship. Agrippina seeks desperately to steer her ship over the treacherous sea of passions, but she gives herself to the elementary abyss of life in order to safeguard her existence. And out of these elemental depths arises the dubious life-force like something awesome and demonic. Acte, a favorite of Nero, is stunned and worried by Agrippina's new erotic aggressiveness and talks of this "unnatural" nature as if in the queen's case it is *supernatural,* a magical force (III, 78–81). The familiar metaphoric "fire" flames up with full significance both as passion and as an agency of doom. The second chorus of *Sophonisbe,* indeed, states that beauty is an incarnation of a magic attractiveness and love a divine principle moving the world, and this idea assumes great importance in the story of Nero's mother, especially at the play's close, as we shall see. The love-making of Poppaea and Agrippina serves clearly as one of the motors of Roman political development.

If one compares Lohenstein to his contemporaries John Dryden (1631–1700) or Jean Racine (1639–99), it is evident

that his freedom in depicting the seduction scene in Nero's
bedchamber actually links him to earlier drama, especially the
cruel realism of the Elizabethan stage, as, say, in the works of
John Webster (1580?–1625). Preoccupation with death and
destruction is evident in the images used by both mother and
son, which despite all rhetoric are quite specific, sensuous, and
unashamed, so much so that many critics have rejected this
incest as distasteful. John Ford's *'Tis Pity She's a Whore*
(1633) treats passionate incest between brother and sister and
approaches the subject as violently, but seems rather wholesome
in comparison, because it is a play about genuine and tragic
love. In *Agrippina*, however, the heroine is not shown to be
pitiful because she is attracted to forbidden love nor idealized
as a sufferer from the point of view of the heart; she is not in
the least enamoured of her son. She struggles, on the contrary,
to subdue a hated monster, lest he assassinate her on behalf of
the adventuress Poppaea. Lohenstein steps out of the shadow
of any puritanical inhibition when dealing with demonic passions. His obsession with the historicity of destructive impulses
drives him to stage even pornographic details. History verifies
the wildest picture of Neronian eroticism; and, therefore, the
facts of destructive passion supersede all interest in the heart
or love, as these appear in the case of Racine's *Phèdre*. Both
playwrights maintain that the passions cause disorder and that
vice is deformity; yet, comparatively, Agrippina and Nero
exhibit scarcely any but monstrous faults, while Phèdre appears
guiltless but damned before the secret court of the human heart.

It is not sufficient to explain that Lohenstein, as a "polyhistorian," is brutally indiscriminate; rather, we must accept, for
what it may be worth, that history *is* his grand authority and
that no other mitigates his portrayal of the perverse world with
its irrational eruptions and catastrophes. Racine's mythologically
and historically grounded tragedies would often still have made
much sense to the ancient Greeks, but Racine was a French
gentleman and, as he said in the preface to *Phèdre* (1677), he

has "amended the authorities." In Racine's case, however profoundly felt, the ancient "story" had to be reconciled with a
second, modern authority, which required a less violent, less
reprehensible heroine. In fact, Racine usually assigned to a
servant, like Oenone, the baser qualities, while Lohenstein gets
along without the *alter ego*. Early psychological novels like the
Princesse de Clèves (1678) demonstrate amply what Racine's
other authority was: a new ethics of nobility for tender hearts.
Out of Christian and stoic origins, as well as the aristocratic
love tradition descended from the Middle Ages, was budding
the ideal of the "beautiful soul." As we have noted, eighteenth-
century sensibilities fastened on Lohenstein's *Ibrahim Bassa,*
which derives from a French source and unites a sentimental
and a spiritual story, because it seemed "inward." The new
age could tolerate and forgive introspective Phèdre's anguish,
the rhetoric of Gryphius, and even *Ibrahim Bassa,* but Lohenstein shocked tender souls by allowing some tragic stature to
Agrippina's immoral struggle in extremity.

The seduction attempt represents the actual turning point
in the queen's drama; and from the middle of the third act on,
she has lost control of the situation, whether or not she knows,
forever. Thus the further subject of the play is really the
approach of inevitable failure and death. These themes are
frighteningly clear in her specious proofs, based on a mechanistic view of the universe, to win over Nero. He fears that
his mother's incestuous behavior is against nature and that the
"beast," as he puts it, if given free rein, will plunge its rider
into an abyss of sin (III, 160). Foolishly Agrippina contradicts
his last flicker of belief in natural law and strives to destroy
in him the restraining taboo. In presuming, desperately, that
she will gain control over her son, she helps undermine the last
bases of possible protection for herself. Her definition of love
differs little in substance from what Lohenstein considers in
the second chorus of *Sophonisbe*. Fated passion, necessary love,

is the motor in a world devoid of any God as prime mover. A melancholy system of immutable destiny prevails in the clockworks universe described by Agrippina:

Einfältger! Wer gibt dir so albre Fabeln ein?
Worwider Stern und Welt selbst müssen Zeugen seyn.
Wir müssen die Natur der Dinge Zirckel nennen.
Denn würde nicht ihr Lauff zu seinem Uhrsprung rennen/
So würd ihr Uhrwerck bald verwirrt und stille stehn.

(III, 179–83)

This advocacy of a return to her womb is laden with morose connotations of doom. A non-Christian, pagan, cyclic view of the world, with history as the ticking of time in a gigantic, rationally perceived process, does not hide the function of irrational drives within this process (III, 214–22). If, as Seneca has already said, shame and taboo are rationally conceived and only "beclouded" eyes cannot see this (III, 64), Agrippina's perverted struggle is all the more futile, for she believes that she is acting rationally, with calculation, in her plan to turn her son against reason. Here we witness the fallacy of unnatural, political existence, which rests on the inherently contradictory principle that man can manipulate or control the mysterious process of the world, into whose captivity he is born for an unavoidable destiny.

A timely interruption by the worried court prevents any successful seduction. When Nero recovers from the spell of his mother, he is revolted by her attempt. The courtiers, now that they know to what lengths she may go in her personal struggle for recovery of power, make Nero pale before the thought of her will. When he begins with them to plan her death, we realize how unavailing her stand has been from the start, for the game turns decisively about. From this moment on, despite any more planning on the part of Agrippina, because she trusts vainly in her ability to survive and in her cunning, when in reality she is nothing more than the out-witted, outplayed former potentate, we look less on her as an evil mother. She has become the victim of her own gamble, and accepts her son's invitation to a love tryst in blissful seclu-sion from the court in a place reachable only by water, even though her aversion to water has been thus far synonymous with survival (III, 373). The deceived deceiver believes in her son's acting of the role of lover. And thus her embarkation upon the sea, in a trick ship so constructed that it will fall apart, is both the symbolic *and* the real equivalent of her leaving firm ground, venturing into the realm of the passions, traveling in dangerous cunning over the abyss. Lohenstein, with masterful irony, makes the favorite rhetorical images of the perilous ocean quite concrete—but thereby changes Agrippina's role within this drama. Now she struggles with blind hope, growing to heroic and tragic stature in proportion to the futility of her position. He has achieved this stature for her without one con-cession to moralistic rules, without diminishing by one iota her guilt and illicit behavior. He sees in her desperation alone the motive for tragedy and the grounds for a tragic conception of man. Neither the weapons of passion nor the manipulations of reason can insure her against the dangers of earthly life—and now there is no recourse, as there was with Epicharis, to a higher instance for salvation. Agrippina's hour has struck; her role in Rome is finished. Agrippina suffers, then, as does Cleopatra in the African play, despite her attempt to use reason to her own advantage.

The third chorus is worthy of special note not only because as a narration it contributes to the flow of the play's action, but also because it celebrates the figure of Agrippina. Two groups, sea and mountain divinities, report in strophe and antistrophe the events on the water during the shipwreck of Agrippina. Only the modern moving picture could, of course,

stage the tempestuous events; for the drama, poetry must paint
them, and a report is necessary. It could be given from within
the play's action, let us say, by an observer of the scene from
an imagined hill or simply related after the fact by the traditional messenger of Greek and French literature. But after
the heated pitch of the third act, with its seduction and deception, the author prefers a lyric transition to lift the audience's
senses to apprehend the terror and raging of the "storm" which
threatens the royal mother. This personification of nature sets
the natural events even more obviously as objective parallels
to the subjective events that transpire in the world of passion.
Nature even interprets the significance of its own reactions as
well as the significance of the disaster; it hastens to point out:
"The Vices are the real winds of shipwreck" (III, 485). In
this chorus Lohenstein demonstrates the intricately conceived
connection between his rhetoric and the substance of his drama.
A "staged" natural setting makes sententious remarks by using
images taken from its own realm, terms already familiar on the
lips of the human actors—the water metaphors which one finds
everywhere. Thus, not only does "water" serve as a metaphoric
system to express the concepts of Fortune and of Passion, it also
plays a "role" factually as the agent of these, a role which merges
metaphor and reality, rhetorical pathos and perceived verities.

The chorus increases our awareness of witnessing a famous
spectacle of history. Nature itself becomes a symbolic theater.
Personified, it takes upon itself the job of preserving the
memory of the event; its "mute tongues" (III, 525) will sing
of the perilous night. Thus the very features of natural things
reveal certain historical truths. The flood, the shifting element
which washes away all forms of existence into the amorphous
oblivion of time, will not annihilate this moment, this spectacle
of wrecked majesty, "will not consume this memory" (III, 524).
The poet virtually promises that the greatness of Agrippina
cannot vanish. Through reference to the famous myth, the birth

of Venus from the sea, this thought broadens into a triumphant rescue of her existence from the engulfing shapelessness. Agrippina comes, like the goddess, back to land. Her attractive form re-emerges from amorphous nothingness, as the incarnation of a principle out of the ever shifting waves of time. In using the metaphoric system of water, Lohenstein progresses from a purely narrative function for it, linking the third and fourth acts, to the function of objective correlation between the concrete and metaphysical phenomena of the drama. Then, with the authority of literary tradition (birth of Venus), he overcomes the metaphorically developed spectacle of temporality, destruction, and oblivion for man; out of this spectacle a new truth of immortality comes. The natural divinities rejoice in Agrippina's rescue. Even though they represent, metaphorically, the threat to her, they praise her intrinsic attractiveness.

One suspects neo-Platonic influences behind these statements. Although the queen is doomed and must be claimed by the forces of time, Lohenstein pauses a moment, allowing her a last victory. Through poetry he redeems her as the eternal Venus principle. He lifts the curse of death for a few seconds to indicate the other, permanent dispensation through fame (recorded ostensibly by nature but actually by art), as we hear in nature's prayer to the night and to the emblems of an eternal order:

> Du braune Nacht die du steckst Agrippinen
> Gestirnte Todes–Fackeln an/
> Dein Schatticht Sarch sey weg gethan/
> Die Sternen solln zu Freuden-feuern dienen.

> (III, 511–14)

The stars as fires of joy point toward immutable greatness. Here the literal meaning applies, too, for the stars shine brightly to illuminate her landing, as the techniques of the seventeenth-century illusionary stage could simulate. But behind the scenic actuality one detects also an old conceptual pair, death and fame, and must conclude that the deeper purpose of the choral narration has been to celebrate in a poetic interlude the rescue by art of a majestic form, to proclaim Agrippina's salvation through a memorial of her experience.

Rescue from shipwreck has made Agrippina all the more terror-struck with a sense of defeat and with anticipation of death. Sorrow has become the inner characteristic of her isolation and fall, the image of her heart: "Bestürtzte Trauer–Nacht! Du Abbild meines Hertzen" (V, 1). She sees herself as the victim of her son's absolute rule (V, 28–30) and thinks of her escape from the sea as an act of godly vengeance, saving her for worse torments (V, 41). In the hour of nemesis, Agrippina is obsessed by memory of her past crimes. They are many and heinous, and their punishment must be accordingly severe. But by now her violent and lustful career, the remembered monstrosity, contrast vividly with the loneliness and guilt of the defeated woman. She has dared to go to extremities and therefore now suffers in extremity, so that we sympathize, as with Lady Macbeth in the hour when past evil haunts her. Agrippina is conscious of her wicked son as an instrument of faceless influences, of numerous political intrigues, persuasions, plans, for which she represents an impediment and which consequently maneuver to destroy her. As a heroine she stands uniquely apart from Phèdre; her crimes are as real as Lady Macbeth's, as likewise are her terror and guilty conscience. And she is quite aware of her political doom, for not moral guilt alone but also political guilt acts as ultimate avenger of her sins. Lohenstein has succeeded in doing that which the second chorus has intimated. He has united the drama of family crime and curse with the drama of historical fate. Predestined, and yet guilty— the tragedy of nemesis. Agrippina now meets her murderers with the profound knowledge of her destiny:

Itzt ist die Stunde dar
Die mein Verhängnüs hat den Sternen eingschrieben/
Eh als mein Lebens–Kwäll im Hertzen ist beklieben.
Diss ist der Tag/auf den der Tod mich hat betagt/
Wie der Chaldeer Witz uns leider! wahrgesagt.

(V, 92–96)

Anicetus, Nero's flatterer, judges murdered Agrippina with the terminology of rationalism. He sees her as the Cartesian animal which has presumed to challenge the universal mechanism with an inferior, subjugated mind:

Nun ligt das stoltze Thier/das aufgeblassne Weib/
Die in Gedancken stand: Ihr Uhrwerck des Gehirnes
Sey mächtig umbzudrehn den Umbkreiss des Gestirnes.
Hier fällt der grosse Stern; Der sich der Sonne schien
Des Römschen Käyserthumbs hochmüthig vorzuzihn/
Vom Himmel ihres Throns verächtlich zu der Erden.

(V, 160–65)

Discounting the speaker's malicious and derogatory intent, we must still admit that her tragedy does demonstrate human reason's failure to control fate. In the stereotype seventeenth-century view, man is divided: on the one hand, he is a mechanism of impulses, drives, passions; on the other hand, he possesses spirituality, the directive power of reason, and aspiration to the stars. Only the explanatory Christian concept of God redeemed this split creature from being tragic by definition. Critics like Schaufelberger have seen the terminology of such dualistic psychology in Lohenstein's works and concluded hastily that in them reason is positive, redeeming, and non-tragic:

Bei dem vorwiegend rationalen Charakter der Ichbewusstseins kann es nicht weiter verwundern, wenn alles Irrationale, das sich dem Zugriff des Rationalen entzieht, nicht als zum Ich im engeren Sinn gehörig empfunden wird und daher im letzten Sinn bedrohlich erscheinen muss. Letztlich vermag nur die Ratio die Existenz des Individuums zu garantieren, da nur in der bewussten und erkannten Sicherheit die letzte Gewissheit, nach der das barocke Individuum strebt, zu verwirklichen ist.[39]

This opinion certainly leaves out of account those criminally tainted heroines who *use* reason deliberately but unsuccessfully in order to survive (Agrippina, Cleopatra). Whether the playwright sees reason as a guarantee depends largely on the context for man, i.e., on the ruling power of man's universe. Rütsch insists that a transcendental irony of theodicy is the *sine qua non* for seventeenth-century theater, and therefore excludes Lohenstein, because world-theater *should be* an expression of theodicy; Gryphius, of course, fits:

Auch Gryphius gehört von unserm Aspekt aus in diese Ordnung. Lohenstein dagegen steht ausserhalb, er hat den hier vorgebildeten neuen Heroismus in seinem Formalen isolisiert: seine Helden erhalten sich nicht aus der Hand Gottes zurück, sondern sie treten sofort absolut als solche auf und ermangeln eigentlich eines Gegenspiels.[40]

This indirectly contradicts the sort of conclusion reached by Schaufelberger and is most revealing, since Rütsch really rejects Lohenstein because he is a tragedian; tragedy is supposedly not "baroque":

In diesen Formen wandelt sich im Barock eine eigenartige folgerichtige Dramatik ab. Sie ist nicht tragisch, sie hat statt der Tragik den Gehalt der Theodizee. Diese erhält eine Kraft

zum Drama aus dem aufstrebenden Individualismus, der sich
ihr als Partner entgegenstellt und seine Auseinandersetzung
mit ihr austrägt im Schauspiel des gespannten Gleichge-
wichts, im Trauerspiel des Gerichts, in der Tragikomödie der
Verwandlung.[41]

Not pursuing this "exception," Rütsch ignores altogether the
possibility of tragedy.

What is interesting about Lohenstein is precisely that he
does apply the psychological terms of his day but offers no
solution to the questions of existing evil and enslaving temporality. While his dualism and tragic sense derive from the
Christian tradition, especially from the obsessive question of
free will versus predestination, it is through his rationalistic
dissociation from the theology that he arrives at a view of
tragedy as the *drama of temporality itself*. Time is unmasked as
unredeemed, replete with violence and madness; that is why,
when Agrippina hears the approach of the assassins, she cries
out: "Mad play of time!" ("Verrücktes Spiel der Zeit" [V,
111].) His analysis of man under dualistic categories leads to
profoundly pessimistic discoveries, perplexing irrationality in
man and in his world. Doubtless his treatment of despicable
antiheroes reflects these explorations.

Agrippina ends not only with the queen's tragedy but also
with the sentencing of Nero to mental torture. Nero becomes
more terrifying through his perplexity with crime and his in-
ability to expiate. Conscience looms up in the fourth act hand
in hand with forewarnings of doom for the guilt-ridden emperor.
The ghost of Britannicus appears on stage before the sleeping
man to give a picture of the inner visions, fears, and torments
which plague the monster. When he awakes from this nightmare, which represents his soul, he no longer speaks with
pompous assurance as in the first act; all his human frailty and
trembling expose themselves. Nero's mind houses demonic

deformities which gain more and more control over his behavior. With no inner resources, he quivers in encounter with Agrippina's ghost, who accuses him of dishonoring her grave and condemns him to suffer forever pangs of conscience, unless he appeases her spirit. Burrhus comes upon Nero ready to kill himself for peace. The emperor's conscience swells with torment and paranoiac imagination; for him the night hides enemies, and he believes the army wishes to murder him. If Nero finally turns to magic, it is because he feels no security in the world, no trust in nature. The magician's invocation of the dead woman leads not to reconciliation but to mental shock. Nero faints at the apparition of his mother and imagines falling into an abyss. In the seduction scene he has already feared this plunge. This is a monster, but this monster suffers. And Lohenstein tells us plainly that there is no possible escape for him from his abyss, not through reason, for he does not rule over his own mind, not through irrationality, for his chaotic impulses cause only worse pain, and not through supernatural help, for no God intervenes and no magic powers work against the *facts* of nature.

The final chorus presents the spectacle of his mind, the story of eternal damnation, which the furies and the spirits of Orestes and Alcmaeon act out. Lohenstein warns against meddling with the abyss (V, 788–90) and demonstrates the nightmare of conscience (V, 855–56). Clearly the abyss, spawning lust, incest, murder, and madness, is a fountainhead of fate. No longer does the bright ideal sphere of *Epicharis* nor the unshakable love of Ibrahim and Isabelle represent exclusively the mysterious welling of destiny. Lohenstein is concerned deeply with the question of violence and crime, which he re-explores most thoroughly in the helpless depravity of Ibrahim Sultan, his last original inspiration for the drama, if one considers that *Cleopatra* and *Sophonisbe* have their roots in the same creative decade as *Epicharis* and *Agrippina*. Feminine grace is one of the constants of the universe, a neutral and rationally perceptible part of our

73

world. It is, however, often tragically the excitant lever which triggers off inside the human animal a "mechanical" response— in contrast, let us say, to a "spiritual" response. As the essay has pointed out, Ibrahim Sultan reacts to Ambre as a beast would, while the Begler-Beg responds in an altruistic and noble manner. All the rational condemnation of the former's wild urges does not, nevertheless, detract from our sympathy for him as a driven man. Lohenstein may not have gone as far as Shakespeare and made some equation between character and destiny, but he has certainly indicated in the case of weak Ibrahim an internal source of disorder. The world is an ambiguous stimulator, but the ultimate origin of Ibrahim's trouble is within, is his internal chaos, his lack of rational guidance.

The play's psychologizing tendency and pessimism are representative of a basic drift from the position of the earliest drama with its unquestioned absolute values. *Ibrahim Sultan* clearly reveals Lohenstein's special interest in the uncharted abyss of the human mind, whose mysteriousness seems to imply something unfathomable about the entire universe. The prologue hints at a natural analogy between abysmal processes in the world and in man, its microcosm (line 6 ff.), and during the visitation of the fourth act, Amurat's ghost makes the comparison outright:

Man misst mit Bley des tieffen Meeres Grund/
Durch Glass erforscht man's Himmels Heimligkeiten;
Kein Schau–Glass nur/kein Bley–Maass ist uns kund/
Die Nachwelt wird auch keines nicht bereiten/
Das der Menschlichen Gemüther tieffes Welt-Meer gründen kan.

(IV, 263–67)

As we have said, the "rational" pious heroine Ambre excites bestial passions in this blindly floundering tyrant, who under-

74

mines his own crown and sanity. As a result, however, of the
revolution which she inspires, the play ends not just with the
radiance of a new coronation but with a final terrifying descent
into the depths. Going mad in the dungeon, Ibrahim fights
specters and is strangled. There is no doubt that he is a negative
example, like Nero, an antiheroic monster whom we are supposed to watch being caught in the toils of darkness. But the
play blots out the stereotyped appeal of the light. Although that
appeal may be intended, strong irrational impulses counteract it.
We see a real monster; yet this monster suffers, and his suffering commands the scene. Lohenstein dwells on every step of his
fall, because this is the pattern of true tragedy: "Doch diss ists
Vorbild nur des rechten Trauer–Spieles" (V, 451).

He seems to be reaching for a new position where, like
Shakespeare, for instance, he can create tragedy based on the
weakness of man rather than upon his strength *(Lear)*, upon
his immorality rather than his morality *(Macbeth, Richard III)*,
and upon his collapse rather than upon his perseverance when
bludgeoned by chance. But, of course, this drama is still vastly
different from the Elizabethan. The already deposed ruler who
performs empty gestures approaches the Shakespearean vision
of man the futile actor, so bitterly and nihilistically stated by
Macbeth in his final hour of existence ("out, out . . . "), but
Ibrahim has no last strong spite in him. And if his blindness has
captured our attention, and his abject station finally strikes us,
he is not redeemed by any good qualities as was Lear. At the
time of crisis, the sultan becomes a ludicrous actor, a blind man
playing out a show over which he imagines he is still judge, so
that he appears to be rather almost a pitiful victim to the system
of power and to the shift in the constellation of this power.
While civil and ecclesiastical authorities formulate a concept
of law under which they can judge their monarch, a law based
on plain political necessities, he continues to parade in the role
which no longer factually exists. The mask, his state function,

passes to others who bestow it upon a new ruler, and only the stripped human being remains, laden with all the crimes which his political existence has allowed, has even tempted him to commit. The naked guilty man finds no garment of majesty around him to cloak the abyss of his nature. Instead he awakes into the world as into a dark prison-house, filled with specters of doom and the horrors of madness. Ibrahim Sultan's career fits part, but only part, of the pattern in Calderón de la Barca's (1600–81) *La Vida es sueño*. We learn that he has emerged from the dungeon and misery to absolute rule, which is his testing ground, and for there, in failure condemned again to nothingness, returns to his origin. What is lacking is precisely Calderón's theodicy. The hero may not benefit from the "nightmare" of life and kneel finally in prayer, awake, intent upon the seriousness of his role; there is no ultimate redemption.

It is well to emphasize also that the state is *not* portrayed as holy or ordained. It is simply there—a combination of what today we might call "interpersonal relationships." Nor is Lohenstein advocating the rights of a natural political entity, as opposed to the divine right of kings. The Turkish state is a convenient mirror of realities which he perceives in the political structure of his world in general. He peeks behind the sacramental trappings and buttressing rationalizations of authority in *Ibrahim Sultan,* a play which exposes through violent contrasts the hollowness of the outwardly splendid and "rational" events of the grand world in the higher spheres of religion and government. The second Turkish drama alternates the dazzling spectacle of a coronation with the dark scene in a dungeon, and almost all discussions of law, right, tradition are balanced by naked acts of violence. Thus the fourth chorus claims bitterly that corruption and treachery lurk under the sacred regal or pontifical robes; all the outward glory masks the hideous inner truth:

NIm du den Rock des allgemeinen Heiles/
Gürt über ihn des rechten Eyfers Schwerdt.
Wer meynte? dass der Aufruhr meistentheiles
Gekrönte Köpfe so-vermummt verzehrt?
Hierinnen kan ein Stifter Mord– und Brandes
Ein Schutzherr seyn/ein Vater's Vaterlandes.

TIsiphone/zeuch an die Priester–Kutte/
Nim die geweihte Fackel in die Hand.
Wer dächte? dass die Infel schwer von Blutte/
Diss Rauchfass wer' ein Kwell voll Gift und Brand.
Diss Mummwerck kan als heilig dich erheben/
Wirstu gleich Gift im Himmelbrodt eingeben.

(IV, 507–18)

Naturally, the drama is conceived as a warning example, the
"negative" mirror for princes. But its negations apply nonetheless to that which is "Turkish" in Europe—now including church
and state!

In dealing with Agrippina, Lohenstein is more interested in
her struggle, although he shows the corruption of her world in
detail. Through her activity, futile as it may be, and through
her connection with the Venus principle, she attains some
stature. The failure of her calculations, which indicates the
foundering of reason, fits the usual tragedy of the fall of the
prince, especially the criminal prince. But Ibrahim demonstrates
a horrifying lack of wilfulness; whence then his hubris? He
yells that he would rather die than return into the darkness of
prison, yet begs to be put into the nearest cell when he believes
he must otherwise really be killed. This grovelling and broken
figure, once a king, disappears into physical and spiritual depths,
beset by oncoming madness and guilt, cursing the remote outside world, trying to resolve to kill himself rather than suffer

shame. He grasps for stature, sounding in the dungeon momentarily like a martyr:

> Ein selbst-erkiester Tod ist rühmlicher und besser/
> Als der Tyrannen Spiel/der Hencker Opffer seyn.
>
> (V, 756–57)

Thereby he is all the more pitiful, for he cannot find any means with which to kill himself and starts beating his head against the wall. Ambre's ghost intervenes and states that he may not be granted even the slightest reprieve, not even self-inflicted death. In this instant, then, Ibrahim's guilt passes beyond the ordinary sphere of moral condemnation into the amoral, inscrutable framework of nemesis. He cannot help himself through any voluntary act. When the executioners enter, the mutes who strangle political prisoners, Ibrahim sees the spirits of murdered bassas come to watch accusingly; and in his ultimate terror he asks to be choked rather than have to bear the presence of ghosts any longer. The human mind has become something very different from the repository of unshakable ideals, as in the first Turkish play or *Epicharis*; it is also the gateway into time, for eruptions of some frightful nightmare, a terror which seems attached to life. Ibrahim's hubris seems, in the final analysis, to have been born.

When Lohenstein returns to the Turkish themes, he plumbs the negative depths of his Christian origins. If we may be permitted a comparison for this rationalistic, worldly drama, then the inexorable collapse of the sultan suggests original sin, that grim hopelessness of a world peopled in the majority by the unfortunately damned predestined souls of Calvinism, while the stubborn wilfullness of Ambre is analogous to absolute, militant commitment, as made famous by the Jesuits. These types tend to remain poles apart in Lohenstein's inferior dramas, although Agrippina offers an exception. We shall now turn to Lohenstein's best plays, the African tragedies, where both heroism and villainy characterize more dynamic protagonists.

Chapter Five

LOVE AND POLITICS

THE GENERAL TREND in Lohenstein's dramaturgy from the antiheroic type of the 1660's to Cleopatra and Sophonisbe (1680)
is evident in two versions of the play *Cleopatra*.[42] First of all,
the expansion of the fifth act by some three hundred and fifty
lines indicates the importance of her death. Its second scene,
increased by one hundred and eighty lines, allows a direct confrontation with Antyllus, the grown son and natural representative of Anthony. At first Antyllus curses her, but overcome by
her motherly and pious attitude in the face of death, accepts
that she has changed and revokes the curse. The earlier version
avoided staging as much detail and merely reported Antyllus'
assassination; thereby the original fifth act gave greater emphasis
to Augustus' reactions to these happenings than to the attitudes
of the expiring queen and her party. The final tribute is also
rewritten; a new fifth scene of about two hundred lines closes
the story of the unique, ancient kingdom of Egypt and simultaneously its final, exotic chapter—Cleopatra's reign. The effect
is similar to that of the first version. By honoring her tomb and
that of Alexander the Great exclusively, Augustus elevates his
escaped prey to a special status. He sends the dead queen's
earrings to the temple of Venus in Rome, and this act expresses
the awe which even his rational mind experiences before the
manifest power exercised through Cleopatra by this goddess.
Like Agrippina, the Egyptian is exciting even in death, and
Augustus marvels over her regal beauty and feminine triumph.
The enlargement upon her dying is paralleled by another
change. In the first version, Cleopatra was not as sharply drawn

early in the play as a calculating woman who worked toward a single political goal. Instead, she had the shading of an Agrippina, some touch of genuine fear of treachery. It was almost as if, through blinding anxiety, she failed to comprehend Anthony's true character and, for this reason among others, was tempted to negotiate criminally with the enemy. Version two shows her, however, in a secret session with Augustus' emissary in the first scene of the second act; this negotiation makes it plain that she has been considering the removal of Anthony even before the stormy session of his advisers who impugn her value and loyalty.

Despite the big difference in her political clarity and deliberation, Cleopatra remains in the general situation of Agrippina—a seductress at the end of her powers, too ready to engage in immoral adventure, but doing all for the sake of survival. What really gives significance to this shift of emphasis is a complementary delineation of the hero. By making the tragic helplessness of Anthony so obvious, Lohenstein changes the entire balance of the play and, simultaneously, Cleopatra's role. The first act is wholly rewritten. The new materials, especially Sertorius' embassy (the third scene, repeated in the second act, sixth scene), stress Anthony's loyalty and inner exhaustion. He cannot abandon the queen and is not strong enough to flee to a new refuge, Iberia, in order to carry on the fight for noble liberty. Antyllus reveals, at the end of the revised first act, that Thyrsus has transmitted treacherous proposals to Cleopatra, but this accusation cannot shake his father's conviction. Thus the contrast is much stronger in the opening of the second act, when we again see Cleopatra, now actually receiving Thyrsus' next embassy. We know at once that her warm, feminine behavior in the first act, in which she plays the part of a distraught wife terrified at the prospect of abandonment, has been just marvelous acting. She does not plunge into desperate action because of any possible moral shortcoming in Anthony, but is a wily dissembler. From the very start she has seen herself in a role, that

of a calculating mind pitted against a most awesome enemy, fate.
She tries to interpret all the signs in the world drama, and fate
seems to have marked Anthony for failure. Mistakenly, however,
she thinks that these indications are applicable only to him and
tries to evade destiny, which operates in the guise of the Roman
empire and Augustus.

The three queenly tragedies, *Agrippina, Cleopatra,* and
Sophonisbe, have in common a rapid initial start, the precipita-
tion of crisis, in combination with the delayed appearance of
the female protagonist. The first act of the revised *Cleopatra*
opens at the moment of virtual defeat. The historical circumstances and events which have led to the impasse are not acted
out on stage but are only reported, and for Anthony the play
begins, then, at once as a play of nemesis. In flight and despair,
cursing a power that is invincible, he exhibits a considerable
consciousness of history in the opening lines:

> KEhrt Rom den heilgen Nil nun in ein rothes Meer?
> Fleusst nichts als Bürger–Blutt statt fruchtbarn Wassers her/
> Wormit die Tiber wird ersäufft/der Phrat beflecket?
> Die Gräntz ist der Natur/der See ihr Ziel gestecket/
> Der Schatten misst die Nacht/das Sonnen–Licht den Tag/
> Nichts aber den August. Kein Bindnüs/kein Vertrag
> Ist seiner Wercke Maass. Rom mag die Welt besiegen/
> Er sieget über Rom.

(I, 1–8)

A triumphant principle is on the march, politically as the Roman
state, individually as Augustus; but Rome and Rome's chief are
more than "mortal" opponents. By his brooding and reflection in
the first scene, Anthony stands out as a very human hero, a
man of tested strength but now undermined by weakness. In
contrast, the as yet unseen foe, who cannot be limited in any

conventional way, seems inhuman; in Augustus' relentlessness is the terrifying aspect of a beast of prey, an apocalyptic monster in destructive rage:

Wer wil den Tiger zwingen
Durch Gütte/der bereit in den zerfleischten Darm
Die Klauen eingesenckt? Ha! heiss erhitzter Arm!
Der dem gefällten Wild auch Höl und Nest zerstöret!
Der/wenn der Stamm zermalmt/die Wurtzeln auch versehret
Der/wenn der Löwe Raub und Nägel eingebüsst/
Der Löwin auch die Brust und ihre Jungen frisst!

(I, 16–22)

The kingly lion without teeth and claws—so Anthony, with the pathos of a very sentimental hero, sees his hopeless role as protector of Cleopatra and her dynasty. These Renaissance clichés show the conflict as primeval struggle for mastery, without suggestion of ultimate purposes beyond the facts of life and survival. He refers to a nest, a last refuge, and not to a higher set of values. Anthony is faced simply by the animal instinct and horror of downfall, beleaguered now in his citadel.

Egypt is Anthony's marriage portion; Cleopatra is his consort; the geographical, political, and familial spheres of liberty overlap and are simultaneously ringed by threat. With the ethos of conquest Rome drives toward enslavement of the whole world, and likewise Augustus aspires toward absolute power over all Romans, who formerly enjoyed republican freedom, toward annihilation of political liberties and toward his own emergence as tyrant, as supreme ruler and moulder of history, with command over all individual destinies (I, 8–11). Married happiness in a limited free domain is impossible in the face of Augustus' voracious pretensions. So great is Anthony's despair that he thinks about sacrificing himself for his family and the welfare of all. His initial speeches convey thus the first overtone of his nature as the priest-king who must die, a victim of a historical necessity and collapse of the state. Lohenstein has also achieved an interesting development of the stoic sentimental theme which appeared in *Ibrahim Bassa,* his earliest drama. There pure love was an inner goal of freedom and a higher authority on behalf of which Ibrahim abandoned the state and even submitted to death. The saintly lovers certainly acted through inspiration for private happiness but as subjects in spiritual opposition to the demands of their political ruler. Anthony, however, has started life as a free Roman citizen and a noble and has retreated finally to Egypt, where he still maintains liberty and a share in the direction of government. His love suicide will elevate a quite terrestrial reality, his intimate connection to a beautiful and desirable woman, to an absolute status. He will not die executed on behalf of any idea, as was Ibrahim, but through tragic self-immolation upon the imagined loss of Cleopatra, his personal paradise.[43]

The terms of Anthony's personal situation are made synonymous with the terms of Egypt's extremity. His urge to die, if he followed it, would mean in the opinion of several of his advisers political suicide for the realm. Already, with the insistence on images of sea and harbor, ship and storm, one perceives that a rhetorical proliferation underlies the language of the drama. Anthony's first extensive use of the picture and theme of shipwreck (I, 23–30) is a standard cliché for personal disaster. There persists, however, between the rhetoric and the real situation a more than emblematic relationship; often this relationship proves to be historical irony. Thus it is not surprising, for example, that water metaphors occur so often, since Egypt is synonymous with the Nile and since its life depends on control of access to the sea. Since the characters who use this metaphoric language speak self-consciously as actors performing roles, rhetoric fits their ironic awareness of themselves engaged in an action and frequently underscores the bitter realization that somehow they are caught in struggle against "the topsy-turvy play" ("das verkehrte Spiel" [I, 86]) of the world, that, in fact, they are involved in a universal metaphor. Without religious conviction, they recognize no ultimate reasons and justification for the vicissitudes of history, for personal suffering, for helpless enchainment by the circumstances of nature. Only the awareness of opponent powers and of one's own role remains, a brooding obsession in *Cleopatra*. The harbor is then, literally and symbolically, a refuge. Lohenstein consciously chooses this image, because blockaded Alexandria *is* the ultimate retreat of the "last" free agent resisting the encroachment of Rome, and of Rome's tyrant, upon all liberty. Also, the image of the destroying storm is specifically applicable to the great defeat at Actium, where Cleopatra's fleet fled the Roman sea power and precipitated the total collapse.

It is interesting that when Anthony recounts the defeat at Actium he portrays his hidden enemy, destiny, with the same terms applied to ambitious Augustus. It seems as if the very mood of nature was against him in the sea storm that ripped his fleet prior to the naval encounter. The world is a place, according to Anthony, where fate always has bared its teeth and claws at him (I, 89), but surrender is impossible for the Anthonian type. Determination not to be a spectacle of unworthiness is counterbalanced by joy in one's own identity. And so the actor must play on, achieving affirmation and reaffirmation. With maintenance of role as the highest happiness, a supreme sacrifice is even desirable (I, 147–48); thereby, despite the consciousness of captivity in a role, in decreed circumstances of struggle, the ideal of freedom is upheld:

> Gefahr ist für Gefahr der beste Rath und Pflaster.
> Wie kan dis sicher seyn/was uns die Tugend Laster/

86

Ein Römer knechtisch heisst? Gesetzt/wir fallen hin;
Die Freyheit bleibt uns doch fürs Leben zum Gewien/
Ein nie verwelckend Lob fürs Ungemach zur Beute.

(I, 159–63)

The numerous antithetical statements of defeat as victory, death
as immortality, extinction as a guarantee against time, reveal
an irrational yearning for some resolution. Warriors are distinguished with words usually applied to martyrs and virgins,
"golden lilies of honor," "purple of our blood" (I, 203, 204).
Like the saint, the free man is expected to suffer death rather
than admit base attachment to life. Anthony represents, in these
terms, a pathetic example of division and confusion. He quests
for such purity and permanence *because* of his attachment to
his wife and family. These are the tangible blessings he can
well recognize. Yet, like those heroes convinced of their own
monumentality, who face death with unmistakable pride, Anthony too thinks about his picture (I, 252), his victories (I, 244),
and his lasting memory (I, 232), worries that Augustus is
stealing his fame and seeking to eradicate his memory (I, 255).

It is clear that he is willing to die mainly because he does
not want to abandon his human environment when he does not
grasp the opportunity of flight from Egypt to Iberia in order to
entrench "the free senses" (I, 145) in a craggy exile, as Canidius
already suggests. Anthony calls Egypt the present fatherland of
Romans, that is, of the free, and refuses to abandon it and
Cleopatra. For him the crisis is double. He fights ostensibly to
prevent the eradication of liberty; Augustus' aim is to remove
any refuge from Rome and the last representatives of freedom
(I, 271–72). But Anthony actually needs Egypt to sustain him
vitally, and, as Junius puts it, exile and escape would only
prolong the agony of existence (I, 321). Since he must survive
or perish with Cleopatra, his life is Egypt's. To win his con-

tinued support, Cleopatra's chief minister Archibius emphasizes this bond in words of glory foreshadowing the spectacle of a doomed union:

> Wenn Tacht und Oel entgeht den lodernd-hellen Flammen/
> So zeucht der letzte Strahl die gantze Glutt zusammen;
> Wenn sich der Sonne Rad senckt in die düstre See/
> So sieht man: dass sie erst mit Blutte niedergeh;
> Wenn Seele/Sinn und Geist aus Marck und Adern stertzen/
> So fängt der Tod erst an zu kämpfen mit dem Hertzen;
> So mag/wenn Stadt und Reich mehr keinen Athem hat/
> Die Sonne dieses Reichs/das Hertze dieser Stadt
> Der grosse Fürst Anton mit letzten Tugend–Strahlen
> Der Freyheit einen Sarch/ihm sein Begräbnüs mahlen.

(I, 399–408)

As future events reveal, the emphasis on the heart, characterizing Anthony, is appropriate in more than one way. Thus far, in the first scene of the first act, "heart" summarizes his heroism and his readiness to sacrifice for the commonweal, attributes of a great prince whose magnanimity is thought to derive from the inborn quality of freedom. His "heart" manifests, however, a second fealty which seems most unfree. In every instance, then, the double significance of Lohenstein's dramatic idiom prepares one for a tragic finish.[44]

The Roman and male figure normally should be associated with reason, the Egyptian woman with passion. Outwardly she appears to be, first coming on stage in tears with heated exclamation (I, 462), reporting numerous omens in the temple. Cleopatra's initial appearance is under the sign of the animal gods of Egypt at the downfall of their country. Here one experiences a startling motivating repetition of the paradoxical duality which troubles Anthony. Although the gods stand for the life-forces of the country, their earthly aspect is weighted by dark and mysterious portents. For example, the sacred ox, in which Osiris' soul is supposed to have taken dwelling, goes berserk, hurling itself to extinction. In a frightening example of mysterious madness, the theme of self-immolation, the Roman, Anthonian, or sentimentalized magnanimity unto death, appears in its Egyptian, Cleopatran, or animalistic variation. Anthony's relation to the divinities is well established; Cleopatra is called Isis, he Osiris throughout. As Osiris' soul has entered the animal nature of the ox, so also has Anthony entered the kingdom of animal gods, Egypt. The collapse of the temple's chief representative divinities, Isis and Osiris, is already bemoaned by the priests as a "tragedy" (I, 514–17). Trying to calm such fears, Anthony explains the situation in terms of the familiar duality, reason versus passion, or spirit versus flesh, and himself links the Egyptian problem to the omen:

> Ach! wolte Gott! die Sinnen
> Des Leibes tödteten nicht Muth und Rath in dir!
> Denn Typhon ist das Fleisch/und die Vernunft Osir;
> Was Viehisch in uns ist/ermordet Seal und Leben!
>
> (I, 520–23)

Typhon, the ass, incarnates brainless, vindictive, and stubborn nature. Ironically, Anthony, a Roman who ought to and believes he does uphold the principle of rationality, is operating from within the Egyptian world of animal gods, a realm of the flesh and passion. Yet he refuses to see what Caesarion sees, that "Egypt's decline and end are now come" (I, 546). In the presence of Cleopatra, he grows more and more determined to resist fate and to rally a defense. Under her spell, Anthony becomes blind to the threat and believes in a remote solution.

89

When the remote possibility comes true, when an unexpected turn of fortune occurs which could promise him literal freedom, he falters. As mentioned, the new scene of Sertorius' embassy (I, 590 ff.) sharpens the delineation of character. The Iberian herald of liberty asks Anthony to abandon the debacle of Egypt and lead a fresh cause. This commission restores vitality to the ideal of freedom, for Anthony is faced by real choice. But, as if fate wishes to interrupt the influence of a valid hope, Augustus' ambassador appears to negotiate with the Romans (I, 640 ff.), attempts to split them from their Egyptian allies, and excites Anthony to defense of the queen by his taunts. Roman *ratio*, represented by Proculejus, is not just clear thinking but political thinking *(raison d'état)*; no earthly ties are sacred if political necessity demands their termination. Through the council's deliberations, Lohenstein adds depth to his exposition of Anthony's dilemma. The aspiration for what is a non-political freedom, as in *Ibrahim Bassa*, binds him dangerously. Freedom for the heart is, of course, non-political in respect to the age of absolutism and "tyrannical reason," and especially in this confrontation with hard reality. His officers demand that he "conquer himself" (I, 896–99), subordinate love and beauty because the exigencies of ruling outweigh all other things. In the face of so bitter a choice, which we now recognize is equivalent to parting from Egypt with Sertorius, Anthony begins to emerge as a tragic figure. With absolute longing for loyalty and truth in a world of intrigue and deception, he opposes to the political, as did Ibrahim, a sacramental ideal. In Anthony's eyes the validity of one's love oath is all important (I, 902), and he distinguishes between his political marriage to Octavia and his genuine attachment to the Egyptian queen. Love opens his eyes to ideal conditions of life, to permanence, trust, and "lawful" bonds. In the debate about responsibility for control of one's destiny, Anthony speaks of a realm not governed by reason or time.

Antyl. Gedult/Vernunfft und Zeit schafft endlich
Heil und Rath.

Ant. Nicht/wo Vernunfft und Zeit kein Regiment
mehr hat.
Die Liebe lässt ihr Reich durch Klugheit
nicht verwirren.

(I, 941–43)

This theme of an extratemporal love outside of reason's grasp governs the spectacle of his fall; he acknowledges not a fanciful but, ultimately, a tragic *razón de la sinrazón*.

This "unreason" is most significant in a veteran experienced in the crooked realism of power struggle. The combination of strength (Roman manly virtue) and weakness (Egyptian womanly feeling) makes him more acceptable under, say, Lessing's, neo-Aristotelian definition of the tragic hero as a mixed character; he is so sentimentalized that he no longer fits under Corneille's category of *admiration* as much as under that of *compassion*. Even his love suggests mixture. He combines the steadfastness of an Ibrahim Bassa with the blind helplessness of the sultans, ideal love with passionate bondage (I, 947–50).[45] Seeing himself as a new Paris who is unable to do otherwise, although it mean a fall, he denies (like Ibrahim Sultan) that man's free will can act against fate (I, 959–60); also, therefore, he dissociates himself from any higher spiritual faculty of the stoic hero, such as moral reason (Ibrahim Bassa), from the ideal of freedom, and acknowledges an invincible doom which stands above "reason's" comprehension or control. And yet, Anthony's unconquerable love does not fail in the face of death and he keeps his word that not even the physical removal of Cleopatra would alter his attitude (I, 1012). This operatic theme, the Orphic survival of love over death, substitutes for the martyr's sort of personal nobility through freedom. In other words, Lohenstein creates within the spheres of both *ratio* and *passio* a polarity of base or unsympathetic versus noble or sympathetic behavior rather than use a simple duality of negative versus positive character. Only if impressed by this greater complexity in characterization can we fully appreciate the contradictions in Cleopatra, contradictions which make her one of Lohenstein's two imposing feminine figures. In contrast to Anthony, she tries most deliberately to use reason for controlling her destiny and is, up to the moment of defeat, all calculation. She even uses the power of love against him like a lethal weapon.

Lohenstein strikingly reverses the normal situation of the martyrdom tradition, where the most sensual figures are unreasonable, sometimes insane, tyrants with huge sexual appetites. He flaunts in the play *Cleopatra* a discrepancy in the nature of the protagonists which one does not find in *Agrippina*. Cleopatra's attractiveness is even more perverse, if one considers that she exploits it, not to control a sensual monster, but to undo a helpless hero. Her monologue proves her to be quite conscious of politics as a vicious game and of history as theatrics. All her acting is also on behalf only of a role, her role as queen, and Lohenstein virtually equates her political existence with her histrionic personality. If her role evokes pathos, this happens not simply because the actress, struggling to maintain her regal mask, still seems somehow to have no choice but also because she acts in such a manner as to destroy the sole alternative, which is what Anthony's love represents and promises. While Anthony surrenders to the demands of an inner truth and thereby accepts doom, Cleopatra presumes to employ all the wiles of her considerable talent and long experience in survival against a master player, Augustus, to find a vulnerable spot in the Roman, but to keep up her own guard. The spectators of this drama enjoy the ironic perspective in viewing the game, since they know that Augustus has attempted unsuccessfully to turn Anthony against the queen and that only his loyalty has so far saved her. Her own disloyalty, which exercise of her rational freedom from ties of love makes possible, leads her to use his devotion treacherously and undermine her own state. It is Cleopatra's tragedy that reason is not sufficient to enable her to see every truth in a complicated world of deception, where one can quite rationally miscalculate. For *raison d'état* is based on a fallacious presumption that an individual can control history by manipulating others, and reason overlooks the very principle of freedom upon which it rests. If men can be rationally free, then the persons in one's calculation may be themselves calculators. Reason is overweening when it pretends to usurp the function of fate, the inevitable but noncalculable process in which the many individual apparent freedoms, and likewise the apparent bondages, are all subordinate.

Nor is Augustus, the epitome of the Roman political ethos, intended as a moralistic explanation of success because he is both the darling of fate and shrewder. Lohenstein no longer glorifies love as in *Ibrahim Bassa,* in which it is connected with ideal and absolute freedom; yet one may rightly regard the play *Cleopatra* as a sardonic variation of the old conflict between love and politics. Though reason is the instrument of survival and the political attribute, it is nonetheless blind in its own fashion, blind to a different freedom from historical circumstances. Love, which can never dissimulate, represents this other sphere of freedom. But Lohenstein seems to say pessimistically that neither submission to one's human nature nor the attempt to master and manipulate it changes the outcome. The ideal and absolute attachment to a vision of bliss and permanence, which Anthony shares with the martyr, does not redeem him from the enslavement of passion. The rationality of Cleopatra only draws her into a treacherous whirlpool of time. The distortion of truth, which her game necessitates, is disturbingly ironic in its implications. She reverses all the facts and accuses Anthony of plotting a betrayal; thereby she herself plays a part in what Anthony has called "the topsy-turvy play" (I, 86). Caesarion almost upsets Cleopatra's acting by raising the issue of Augustus' true nature; he claims that Augustus will seek to exterminate him as a son of Julius Caesar and possible rival. Suddenly Cleopatra is enraged because the thought of such treatment stings her pride. Something in her womanly nature responds. The possible transgression upon Caesarion's birthright would be also a crime against her, injury to her motherhood of him by Caesar. She cries out against the suggested monstrous deed by a cousin (II, 208–9).

There are numerous misgivings which one by one reveal more of her positive traits: her worry about Caesarion; pangs of conscience over her dissimulation; fear what the future may say about her, a woman who goes against the law of nature, against her marriage, for political gain (II, 234). Augustus is, despite his greatness or even because of it, inhuman, cold, precise, ruthlessly free from binding laws, a manipulator. Cleopatra begins to feel that heaven will curse her for such a union as she projects. She views the oncoming night as an approach of sorrowful events with the same words which Agrippina used, overpowered by crime and doom: "Bestürtzte Trauer–Nacht!" (Cl., II, 244; cf. Ag., V, 1.) Connected, as priestess and queen, with the cult and politics of the realm, Cleopatra manifests early the first signs of a profounder identity as royal mother and spouse. Thus it is with horrified fascination that one observes the queen, in her long monologue (II, 427 ff.), making her false step in a theatrical world of masks, thinking she can distinguish the faces. In her desperation to save Egypt, she falls into Augustus' trap, believes enough in her ability to utilize the paper promise of a ruthless conqueror, and sacrifices a true, proven husband. Her overweening conception of her own powers, too confident an attachment to a historically outdated identity as enchanting queen, makes her betray herself unwittingly. Cleopatra's hope is based on her past triumphs and not actuality. Not recognizing that her final hour has struck, she concludes that because she can kill Anthony through love she is able to affect the cold Augustus also:

> Denn ist die Kunst nicht gross
> Der/die den Julius für ihr sah kniend ligen/
> Durch süssen Libes–Reitz den Keyser zu besigen.
> Nur Muth! das Glücke spielt/die gutten Winde wehn/
> Und Isis lässt uns selbst ihr untern Schleyer sehn.

(II, 476–80)

The presumption of being able to understand the workings of fate must precipitate a corresponding nemesis. This nemesis becomes the subject of the play after Anthony's tragedy of passion is fulfilled.

All the references to death, fall, and burial take physical shape in the third act, where "appearance" brings us to the brink of reality, as if fate is emerging irrevocably from any and every action that its victims undertake. Anthony is approaching the moment, "where reason and time have no more rule" (I, 942). Death is looming up as the only sure haven, verifying his earlier thought: "Zwei Hafen hat man nur: gewehrt sein/oder todt" (I, 950). And the abyss so often referred to in the first two acts becomes visible, when, in the burial vault of the Ptolemaic line, Cleopatra feigns suicide. For the pageantry of death, she is a consummate actress. But all the clichés of drama, all the rhetorical flourishes, are ironically laden with truth. Almost every lie she tells becomes, because she tries to deceive, a verity. The fake burial rite of the third act is nothing less than a "play within the play," and Cleopatra rehearses what she is to fulfil later as a serious role; without realizing the significance of her behavior, she performs as "theater" the pathetic spectacle of her own factual end and emerges "playingly" in her true part, experiences, despite the present image of herself as a clever actress, the future image toward which she progresses. Her acting is a step in the development of self-awareness. She seems irresistibly drawn toward temple and tomb, irresistibly inclined to take on the role of the dying queen. As in *Agrippina*, we witness "the actor of himself" caught in the play.

As a thematic group, love, death, and fate draw together in the dissimulating speech of Cleopatra (III, 117–21) until self-extinction assumes erotic color. The queen even proclaims that she wishes to marry death (III, 166). Her burial ceremony stands under the signs and auspices of the animal godheads of Egypt, as Lohenstein details them line after line. The sensualism of espousing death is further emphasized by the pageantry and solemnity of the cult. With the emotional language of Christian longing, Cleopatra cries out ecstatically:

> So komm/O süsser Tod/O liebstes Wolgefallen!
> Kommt und erkwicket mich/vergifftete Kristallen!
> Ich küsse Gifft und Glass! *Charm.* Was thut sie,
> > Königin?
> *Cleop.* Was das Verhängnüss heisst. *Iras.* Wo denckt
> > sie/Göttin/hin?
> *Cleop.* Nun in die Ewigkeit.
>
> > (III, 229–33)

Behind the mock stoic drinking of the hemlock and the yearning for eternity, one cannot miss the released nihilism of her exclamation. The "role" is said with too convincing an emphasis of relief: the joy of no longer fleeing fate but of accepting it. The impulse toward destruction, toward freedom from further historical struggle, swells rapturously. Truth shines through all the theatrical costuming of her world, a world sick for death:

> O Nectar unsers Lebens!
> O Labsal unsrer Seel! O Zucker-süsses Gifft!
> Wol diesem! der durch dich so trüber Noth entschifft!
> Der in dein Todten–Bild sein einigs Heil vermummet!
>
> (III, 242–45)

She has not yet fully arrived, however, at the painful stage which we can call "Anthonian." He feels that the frightful vision of cursing ghosts (his victims king Antigonus, Artabazes, and Jamblichus) has been "no false dream" (III, 438). Having become through love a guilty and attached man, Anthony experiences the overwhelming reality of conscience. The visitation and the awakening to find his dagger, placed as if for self-immolation by a supernatural agency—these indicate an irrational welling up of the life-force in the hero which results in his self-destruction. This raging of the life-force is well expressed through the weird occurrences which transpire during his dream and which the watch reports:

> Es war gleich Mitternacht/als Wolck und Himmel krachte/
> Die Erde bebete: dass Stad und Bürger wachte.
> Des grossen Tempels Thor sprang von sich selbst entzwey.
> Nach diesem hob sich an von Bachen ein Geschrey
> Und wilden Satyren/die tausend Fackeln trugen/
> Und hundert Trinckgeschirr in kleine Stücke schlugen/
> Wie wenn sie bey der Nacht Sabazus Fest begehn.
> Ein Esel trug vorher den trunckenen Silen/
> Ihm folgte Bachchus nach bekräntzt mit frischen Reben/

Sein Spiss und Wagen war mit Epheu rings umbgeben/
Vier Luchse zohen ihn durch die bestürtzte Stadt/
Für Maeris Thor hinaus/wo Caesar's Läger hat.

(III, 445–56)

This pandemonium, an apocalyptic vision for a non-Christian
world, should recall the berserk omens in the temple of the
animal gods of Egypt. In the Roman world, Osiris and Dionysius
were associated with sacrificial death, orgiastic rite, intoxication,
madness, and rebirth. When the protective deity, their Roman
equivalent, Bacchus, from whom Anthony is descended, deserts
the beleaguered city and him, Anthony collapses under the
strain of contrary fortune. He knows that his nature is split: [46]

Ich bin dem Vater nach vom Hercules gebohren/
Vom Bachchus aber stammt mein Mütterliches Hauss.

(III, 458–59)

One is familiar with the mythology of a dual nature from
Agrippina, Rubria chorus. In *Sophonisbe* we see the figure of
Hercules, the perfect hero and epitome of virtue (manliness),
who represents proper conduct for a ruler (*So.*, chorus four).
Anthony is outwardly a Roman hero and masculine statesman
with cool self-control, but in him operates a feminine, irrational,
Dionysian impulse, which has bound him to the queen and to
her kingdom of bestial divinities and now casts him down
for ever.

The love-death of Anthony brings final *withdrawal* from
the brutal historical realm into a nihilistically attuned beauty,
infused with religious and erotic fervor; there is a "death aria"
with a dominant theme of marriage which would suit a
Wagnerian music-drama:

98

Cleopatra mein Licht! Cleopatra mein Leben!
Du Seele meiner Seel! umb deinen Schatten schweben
Die Lebens–Geister schon/die mich die heisse Noth
Dir aufzuopffern zwingt. Komm angenehmer Todt!
Erwünschter Jammer–Port! Ich suche dein Gestade;
Wer deine Küsten kiest/der seegelt recht gerade
Den Glückes–Inseln zu. Cleopatra mein Licht!
Ach! ich erblicke schon dein sternend Angesicht!
Schaut ihren neuen Stern in den Saffirnen Zimmern/
Und den verklärten Geist umb diese Pfosten Schimmern;
Hört! wie die Turteltaub umb ihren Buhlen girrt/
Der in der Sterbligkeit ein-öder Wüsten irrt.

. . . .

                nein/bin ich doch bereit/
Der morschen Sterbligkeit meist schon vermodert Kleid
Dem Leib zu ziehen aus. Nicht scheue/meinem Schatten
Den Himmel-hohen Geist der Seele zuzugatten!
Schau doch! ich atheme mehr in dir als in mir/
Komm Schwerdt! komm süsser Todt! vermähle mich mit ihr.

              (III, 545–56, 567–72)

Here is an ecstatic "embarkation for Cythera"; the journey is, of course, the voyage into death, the old Orphic story. His self-extinction impresses itself upon us as an epitome of sacrificial love; he completes his role with a final stroke which makes it a "perfect" work of art.[47] History is theater. In the seizure of love, Anthony's acknowledgment of love represents a choice which has reference to no higher set of values, to no religious principles. The only metaphysics are those of history (existence) and extra-historical permanence (death). He chooses love for eternity; so he wants to be forever remembered—as the hero who chose love at the price of dying. Death is the fixer of roles.

The reversal of the prior news of Cleopatra's suicide demonstrates that Anthony's triumph is permanent. The hero no longer remonstrates against the world; he is not filled with curses against fate; he has found true happiness, which is deepened by the knowledge that she lives. The operatic device of the remeeting of a dying lover and his beloved is intended, as in Shakespeare, to intensify our sense of sorrow over his tragic end; but, in Lohenstein, it also serves for yet another encounter between truth and appearance. One must witness the irreconcilable blindness of love. Now Anthony dares call on once unfriendly gods to give way (III, 656–60), and expires in full confidence of unimpeached devotion. As further proof of his generous nature, his whole attention is focused on Cleopatra and his family's welfare. His only thought for himself is one of final rest. He directs that his body be kept in Egypt according to Egyptian practice. Thus after asking the living to give in to fate, he commits himself to Egyptian, not Roman, earth (III, 730), and so completes his total acknowledgment of his "Egyptian" attachment, transfigured as the victim of this attachment.

The action recommences and broadens into a world perspective. The first emotional climax, Anthony's death, lifts the audience to a high level of awareness; the first three acts serve as the foreplay or fable which gives meaning to the grand gesture by Cleopatra, her suicide.[48] In the fourth act, fate appears in historical costume, through the mask of Augustus; and in the fifth act, Cleopatra answers this direct confrontation. The appearance of the emperor on stage achieves several ends. First, it makes the challenge of fate ever less remote. Second, it reverses the situation of an aggressive, guilty Cleopatra, who finally becomes defensive and, albeit in a different manner, helpless. The splendor of Augustus makes him all the more uncanny in contrast to a sympathetically weak and troubled Anthony; therefore, this next phase of the play, with the glaring contrast of harsh reality, lends the queen a new aura, that of victim. Third, the intrusion of wholly Roman, invading minds places in greater relief the exotic, dark, and unique culture whose special qualities were conditions of the story. These qualities now assume greater importance under the direct threat of extinction. The tables are turned. Egypt has swallowed Anthony, but now Rome swallows Egypt.

Augustus has nothing in common with berserk animalism as represented by the Egyptian cult but possesses all the craft of a great ruler, all the acumen and ready wit of a highly *rational, amoral* character. The scenes in which the general staff discusses strategy show how he masters every event and integrates it into a systematic plot. He exploits betrayed information about Anthony's death to gain an impressive and cheap entry into Alexandria when Cleopatra has hoped to use Anthony's life as a pawn in advantageous negotiations. He releases the hostages, whom he no longer needs; occupies the city, ostensibly in order to protect Cleopatra from lawlessness of the mob; extends amnesty to the Roman troops of Anthony; guarantees the sanctuaries of Egypt; makes other promises of little regard, since he can easily break all; and enhances his reputation as a gracious prince. If Agrippina worries about the political situation in the city of Rome itself which may resist high-handed and independent negotiations by Augustus, the emperor is quite aware of historical necessity, the circumstances of Rome's drive for world domination which necessitate the integration of Egypt into the empire. Lohenstein indeed shows the fusion of all wills in the operation of history, for Augustus is not really protesting the arguments of his officers; pretending to want the nobler and better action, he "accepts" for the good of Rome that which he himself needs to do in order to win a complete and demonstrable victory with trophies and spoils. To show a fabulous queen in chains to the city and to divide the Egyptian treasures is part of his total plan to appease and manipulate

101

Rome. Augustus is not simply adjusting to the exigencies of his historical situation but also calculating far ahead of any other mind what advantage he can obtain through compliance with a given necessity. Through his remarkable statescraft which he lets appear natural or necessary, he keeps his hands on the reins of power. His noble intentions, morality, and reverence are so Machiavellian that one never can be positive where, with him, truth leaves off and theater begins.[49] For example, he does not merely take up the suggestion of Gallus to trick the "worm" with its own weapons, feigned passion (IV, 275–76); he has already carefully prepared for such a strategy—by his secret messages to Cleopatra, by his generous peace terms despite awareness of her weak defenses, ahead of negotiation, and by his steering of discussion in the staff meeting in the direction he desires. His protestations (IV, 238) elicit in his officers agreement with his designs, without their realizing how he guides them. Since the situation is delicate and he worries realistically about his fame, he skillfully transfers any blame for that which he wants onto his council (IV, 301–4).

When Caesarion reports how empty the Roman promises have proved to be, we witness the start of a bitter undeceiving for Cleopatra (IV, 320–22) and of a simultaneous growth in awareness of herself and of her historical identity. She transfers her hopes, even before a last try against Augustus, onto the living symbol of her royal glory—her grown son by the great Julius—and readies herself for sacrifice. Like Anthony, her wish is to preserve freedom for her family, some refuge against time and necessity (IV, 325–27). This pride and memory she cannot allow to be extinguished, so that her affection for Caesarion is also an expression of love for her country, a reaffirmation of her political marriages on its behalf. Thus her farewell mixes maternal with patriotic concern (IV, 383–84). When the Romans of Augustus' staff confront her, the challenge to her greatness is direct. One observes further development of Cleopatra's tragic awareness in her defense of Anthony, whom they

try to defame, thus wounding her (IV, 309–400). Slowly a
new feeling asserts itself in opposition to the Romans. It begins
as a sense of forlornness, which she now must share with dead
Anthony, and demands its own rights against the ethos of cold
statecraft (IV, 403–4). She speaks in the role of the fallen ruler,
as does Syphax at the start of *Sophonisbe*, but also in the role
of widowed queen. Desperately probing and pretending to be
overwhelmed by Augustus' equally feigned amorous intentions,
she rises above her own role, majestically aware now of her
own heart, gambling for a last revenge and the only reliable
solution—death, which will rob the emperor of his triumph and
make her freedom permanent. The queen gathers all her resources as an actress for a final self-assertion that is at the same
time her acceptance of fate.[50] She now deceives the Romans
largely by uttering the truth, as if naïvely hoping. Her fear of
debasement, especially before the eyes of Rome, which is exactly
what the Romans intend for her, restates the dominant theme
of all Lohenstein dramas, the desire for liberty (IV, 421–23,
426–28). In their eagerness to reassure her, they are outwitted
into betraying their actual plans.

Just's interpretation, that Cleopatra woos Augustus genuinely
and that he, the arch-Machiavellian, momentarily succumbs to
her spell, is untenable.[51] One notes that Just prefaces his
thoughts with several questions: whether Augustus is only an
obsessed politician, whether Cleopatra is erotic only in the
fashion of an Agrippina toward him, and other misgivings.
Against the brilliant formulation of Augustus' character by
Lunding, against Oskar Nuglisch's characterization of Cleopatra
as the feminine politician of all times, against his own keen
questions, Just proceeds to the surprising conclusion that the
queen kills herself not to escape captivity (her obsession!) but
the pangs of disprized love, through love's failure.[52] Just overlooks that, if there has been any failure of love's power, this
has already occurred in the relationship of Anthony toward
Cleopatra, although unbeknown to the hero; there is no loving

partner, nor love victim, in the duel between Cleopatra and Augustus. After Anthony's tragedy, prompted largely by his character as a driven man, a new ironic progression toward truth takes place for Cleopatra, clever and penetrating, who can taste bitterly the contradictions in her own position. Although not primarily a reflective, introspective, passive heroine, she is an observer and manipulator who turns at last upon herself in tragic discovery. If there has been any failure of love, and if love has any meaning for her, the mistake on her part has been to squander the sole genuine and sublime passion, and chance for happiness, represented by Anthony.

In her private meeting with the emperor, Cleopatra achieves ultimate mastery in her last performance of the role of deceiving lover, who is, in addition, now aware of having fallen to the deception she practices but of which she is finally undeceived. Although she tries to work her spell as of old and makes a last effort, she is anxiously conscious of age; it seems as if her charm belongs to the past, with Julius and Anthony. Out of her magnificent and amoral duel with destiny, Just makes a tale of rebuffed and unavailing passion! Was he thinking somehow of that other Cleopatra's, the English Cleopatra's, warm heart? Lohenstein's queen does not pretend suicide after fleeing an enraged Anthony, whose mood she would test in order to see whether it is safe to rejoin him; no, she deliberately undoes him; and until her political game is up, she is all deliberation. Only in defeat does Cleopatra understand love and the lost Anthony better, while continuing to loathe Augustus. Acknowledging the finality of her role, Cleopatra does not hesitate longer but feigns obedience and requests a token freedom, a modicum of honor, the right to pay final respects to dead Anthony (IV, 625–30). Thus she brings about her last chance to rescue her identity and achieve realization of Anthony's last wish: royal burial.

The pastoral intermezzo before the final act is not the usual mythological allegory but a distinctly human chorus of simple life close to nature, set in an idyllic garden on the Nile. The mixture of stoic and pastoral reflection is fashionably pessimistic.[53] But Lohenstein has recast the shepherds and shepherdesses of 1661 as the garden folk of 1680, a sign that he regards the pastoral business as too playful for the serious mood. They ennoble natural love, which is pure, and reject courtly, political existence, which is estranged from honesty, nature, and freedom. The sentimental idea that love frees one from bondage in time indicates the widening of the gap between secular Lohenstein and "ethical" Gryphius (*Papinian*, 1659). Certainly the queen is here defended against besmirchment in regard to her final actions; the formula for stature is stated unequivocally: "freedom, death and grave" (IV, 681–84). The equation in *Ibrahim Bassa*, emptied of all doctrinaire content, remains as ultimate explanation. This idealization of natural love is a brief respite from man's artificialities and "play"—a lyric pause which subsides when history and tragedy resume sway. Thus the poetic bridge to the specific and individual moment of freedom for Cleopatra emphasizes the function of the drama; the generic moment—the pastorale—interprets the queen's story as a timeless example. The transition from the chorus' solemn intonement of bliss to the somber splendor of the cult atmosphere is "operatic," because Cleopatra by her very being is theatrical. A new inwardness possesses her, evident in her invocation speech. Through "religious" self-knowledge of role, both as queenly victim and as queenly priestess, she now verifies the sacrifice which previously she had undertaken as deception:

WEr auf das leichte Rad des blinden Glückes traut/

.   .   .   .

Wer viel weiss ausser sich/sich in sich selbst nicht kennet/

.   .   .   .

Der komm und lern allhier. . . .

(V, 1, 4, 6)

Self-discovery, rather than control of outer events, is the final teaching. The drama, then, has exemplary purpose in revealing the necessity of confession of the inner truth—albeit a different truth from that acknowledged by others, like Augustus, Seneca, etc. Acknowledging her great love, which she once betrayed, Cleopatra fulfils the intermezzo's last words about "true fidelity" (V, 13–14).[54]

Lohenstein presents the actual ceremony of embalming with pathological realism, a peculiarly Renaissance fascination for details.[55] Cleopatra expresses *beaux sentiments,* tenderly supervising the grisly operation. Such an incongruous moment destroys the "tragic effect." We mean by this that we resent impediments between our warmer sentiments and their objects; polyhistorical accuracy is not always pretty enough. But, as noted, Lohenstein's authority *is* history. An Egyptian queen would, of course, even passionately desire to embalm her beloved dead. It is likewise historical that incest and murder occurred in the Roman court in Nero's era. We may wonder, nevertheless, how it is that the playwright's characters achieve some sort of insight into their own roles without "seeing" certain horrifying things that they are doing, e.g., inciting to incest. But in tragedy, as in life, such insight seems to emerge with the consequences. In the case of Cleopatra, if she does not "see" the odd fact that she is embalming a body—the peculiar way we might "see" it—that arises from the natural temporal condition which separates, assigns different costumes and roles, according to the thought of the seventeenth century with its grand metaphor of the world as a stage, men as actors. But certainly we may assume that Lohenstein "sees" these mysterious facts. Cold and sovereign mind over the action, he observes and accepts every strange facet of the action. The significance of the burial scene is also, as usual, "fixation" against the power of time. The body is preserved by ritualistic methods to indicate that its spirit is immortalized by fame. Together, the fleshly token and the memory of the dead allow a kind of monumentality that Egypt so remarkably displays in its ponderous tombs and pyramids rising out of the formless desert. This realm of monumentality is timeless, and therefore associated with love, too. Cleopatra begs forgiveness of dead Anthony and asks to remain forever with him in death and be remembered with him. She describes death now as a somber bridal night, with Orphic overtones (V, 38–42).

As mentioned, her evolution as a women has been carefully developed. Now Lohenstein re-emphasizes attachment to her own sons, to Anthony's adult son Antyllus, as well as to her people and country. Her maternal suffering not only partially expiates guilt and modifies her character[56] but also drastically stresses the eradication of the Roman–Egyptian image. Augustus, the determined eradicator, is himself momentarily stunned by the wonder which her "animal" will to freedom has inspired. His question, "What rage, Cleopatra, what fury came over you?" (V, 505), is a final echo of the theme of the raging gods of Egypt, whose temple images have suffered berserk death. Although one is unable to distinguish how much is sincere admiration and how much calculated pose, Augustus knows the proper speech; in any case, a confessional tone would neither suit or convey feelings of a perfect ruler, who shows his own greatness by acknowledging a worthy opponent—whom he no longer need fear. By virtue of acknowledgment, when his re-markable mind projects to see that her memory will outlive even Rome's power, he seals a chapter of history (V, 536–38). He sends the queen's earrings for dedication to the temple of Venus in Rome, so that unmistakably he renders tribute to the eternal principle represented by the goddess and her expired favorite. The picture of the Roman conqueror, all masculine virtue, initiating a new era, shows him at his best without embellishing his innate ruthlessness. With exemplary clarity, he exhibits reverence for the moment of epochal change and worships his-

tory itself. Disdaining to pay his respects to the lesser graves of
the collapsed Ptolemaic dynasty, he pauses only at the tomb of
Alexander the Great. He is the victor and darling of history for
this moment and identifies himself with the archetype of lasting
fame. Lohenstein, who has presented us the tragedy in history,
does not disguise or pass over the other very important reality
of history as victory. But both victory and defeat are subject to
a higher instance: fate. And fame is the only, the amoral, the
necessary answer to a universe without a beneficent deity.

Despite the amazing clarity which is part of Augustus' role,
he does not give the ultimate framework in which his grand
actions are to be seen. All removes again to the abstract plane.
The concluding chorus presents the four rivers, the Tiber, Nile,
Danube, and Rhine, on behalf of three geopolitical and historical
empires. Lohenstein's conception of fate, not as a moral judgment, but as the "arrangement" in the succession of events is
clear from the claim of each falling realm that, while a victim
to change, it is not outshadowed by its follower (V, 801–2).
This depiction of the historical sequence of great powers as a
shifting of vitality leads finally to a tribute to the ruling house
of Austria. Lohenstein's myth of history founders on the shoal
of his own contemporary situation; he cannot, or will not,
project beyond the hoped-for ascendancy of the Germanic
peoples. We find in his age among German humanists an in-
cipient nationalism which frequently betrays, through its anti-
Roman sentiments, a profound sense of cultural inferiority,
jealousy, and ambitious pride. As noted in the first chapter, his
huge novel *Arminius* departs from the plays' more reasoned
assessment of history, without moral aspersions above and beyond
the establishment of the facts of corruption, and indulges in
chauvinistic detraction. The tendency is latent but controlled
in the choral interludes, the only place where German "glory" is
implied, with the exception of Sophonisbe's prophetic apotheosis.
We can say that in so far as such choruses merely flatter a

contemporary audience, they are not integral even to seventeenth-century tragedy. But they have other functions as well. They are a political mirror to propagandize right action on the part of princes and society, and they stir awareness of history as a relentless process of change. The spectator becomes conscious of himself watching a play about a past time, with intrusion of the immediate present and its basis or claim which is rooted in past happening. In Cleopatra, great river systems perform the same role as the empires do in *Sophonisbe* in the final chorus. In startling contrast to the heated emotion of the Egyptian queen's immolation, the long-range historical perspective, with which Lohenstein brackets his drama, sounds lofty and cool. The playwright's return to a sublime vantage point does not, however, come as a shock, if one appreciates the choruses, constant reminders of the "perspective" of lofty, intellectual concepts or principles at play. These various frames for the story—i.e., the specific "history" of the queen and Anthony and Egypt's collapse—intervene regularly, encompass the action, actually constitute an interwoven genre. Just treats structural "interplay" as a stylistic trait of Lohenstein and arrives at some similar conclusions (see his first and third chapters). But Rütsch's book, with its many illustrations of seventeenth-century theatricality, offers better hints as to Lohenstein's dramaturgical impulse. On the one hand, the precise and factually detailed story, on the other hand, the abstract universally perceived principles—these intertwine as an unceasing reminder of the grand metaphor of the world as theater, the performance in costume of a metaphysical drama whose purposes and causes are, however, at least in Lohenstein's works, thought to be remote from mere human understanding. In the final analysis, Lohenstein bows before the unsolved mystery of this drama and seeks, by his great faithfulness in historicity, to imitate the creative process of the world, the process of world-theater, to establish examples which illustrate that vision of acting as existence, role as character, and the play as fate's script. What commentators have several times criticized as obsession with detail, pedantic scholarship, polyhistoricism, is the natural result of the author's fixation upon that metaphorical system of theatrics which besets his age. But it is well to recognize the individual merit of Lohenstein who turned to *historical tragedy* because he came to understand the theatrical process in terms of some fateful "authorship" over the world. Another necessary consequence of his historical-theatrical obsession was a certain introspection in his created characters, who had to conceive of themselves in secular terms of being on the stage of history. They are predecessors of the great self-examiners of much later German dramatic writing.

Chapter Six

GRANDEUR

THE OTHER African tragedy elevating the figure of a fascinating queen is *Sophonisbe,* which Lohenstein may have already begun before 1668 and which he probably wrote in order to commemorate the marriage of Leopold of Austria and the Spanish Infanta in the year 1666. It was, however, first published by Fellgibel together with the revised version of *Cleopatra* in the collection of 1680.[57] No concrete evidence exists whether or not *Sophonisbe,* too, underwent revision. But it is justifiable to accept the date 1680 as the valid demarcation for the play. It exhibits an advanced development of Lohenstein's tragic sense and similarity with *Cleopatra* in choice of historical subject matter and locale. The fact Lohenstein issued simultaneously his reworking of the latter drama and *Sophonisbe* cannot be explained merely as a convenient union. In 1673, the author had published *Ibrahim Sultan,* the frightening spectacle of a ruler's mental and political collapse in confrontation with historical necessity, not simply the story of heroic self-assertion by martyrs against external threats. The descent of the broken king into darkness and extinction contrasted sharply with the coronation of his son, which showed the continuance of the state and of the historical process. Seven years later, and after twenty years' interval between Lohenstein's first African tragedy and its final rendition *(Cleopatra),* other African materials also impressed the author as being suited for publication. The renewed occupation with the African heroine, Cleopatra, may well have summoned Lohenstein to deal once more also with queen Sophonisbe. This pair represent the most mature product of the dramatist, and both are probably reinterpreted figures.

As the opening lines of *Sophonisbe* reveal, the drama is set at an earlier phase in the same historical period which culminates in *Cleopatra*. Whereas in the latter Rome has reached its pinnacle of power and has incorporated the outposts of the world under the aegis of its empire, in *Sophonisbe* one sees the rising power of Rome in the days of pristine, republican vigor, at a crucial turning point in its fortunes, the phase of the Punic wars and conquest of Carthage. Rome reacts positively, as does Hercules so exemplarily in the fourth chorus of the drama, upon the crossroads of decision. The Carthaginian episode also antedates, then, the Neronian episode, in which Rome's rise loses its meaning and direction, in which Rome's process of enslavement of the world has become internalized and Rome's own body politic shows signs of decay. But in *Sophonisbe*, as still in *Cleopatra*, Rome is the starred power which Destiny protects and furthers; and at the play's beginning, it is the shadow of Rome which falls upon North Africa in foreboding of the future. An older civilization, the Phoenician, is on the defensive and in collapse. One cannot separate its death agony from the fate of its rulers.

The action starts, as in Cleopatra, at the end, at the moment of imminent defeat for Sophonisbe's capital city. From its inception the play is an analysis of the stages of hopeless struggle against doom, which stands literally at the gates. Instead of witnessing this collapse from the point of view of the besieged, as in *Cleopatra* through the eyes of retreating Anthony, the reader stands with the conqueror, Masanissa, outside the walls. This difference in the initial situation of the male protagonist is most significant, as later action verifies. Whereas Anthony first appears in flight before and victimized by political aggression, Masanissa is from the start the political aggressor. The former is a political failure, seeking to escape his Roman past and captivated by an African, an Egyptian nature; the latter is a political success, an often passionate African but in process of Romanization. King Masanissa, the ally of Rome, gloats over the revenge he is accomplishing against his fellow African king, Syphax. But underlying his bitter and cruel satisfaction with the spectacle of fires in the city about to fall, there sounds in the very first words of the play, which he utters, his awareness of history as the stage where man, attracted to doom, stands on trial: "Guilt swarms around destruction as moths around light." ("Die Schuld schwermt umb Verterb/wie Mutten umb das Licht" [I, 1].)

Lohenstein uses the same basic images of light and fire so important in *Agrippina*, where a complete mythological fable (in the second chorus) explains the dubious connections between love and the life of the body politic, Rome. Masanissa's statement grimly announces a similar theme of destruction as the result of an inner weakness or proclivity and of doom as some irresistible attractive fire. It is not long until he must overcome such a suicidal attraction in the person of the queen. Lohenstein already casts a subtle veil of irony over the scornful comment by Masanissa; in gloating over the conflagration, he betrays his own fascination with the show of collapse, with the Carthaginian role of fiery consummation. Although the image of fire is not treated expansively in a chorus, it occurs again and again throughout the play up to the moment when Sophonisbe ascends her own pyre, a dominant emblem of collapse. A reader unfamiliar with the mythological prefiguration for Rome in *Agrippina*, the story of Helen and the conflagration of Troy, rightly links the story of Dido and Aeneas, the burning of Cyrtha, Masanissa's temporary weakness, and the funereal arson of Sophonisbe in the fifth act.

There is a difference, however, between the play of crime or sin, *Agrippina*, and the historical plays, *Cleopatra* and *Sophonisbe*. Lohenstein thinks more about the question of state. Syphax' "guilt" in breaking the Roman alliance is, because of his judgment and failure, only historical guilt. He acts wrongly in a period of change so constellated that Rome must win out. Any struggle against her amounts practically to suicide. In this sense, Syphax flies blindly toward perdition, a moth attracted by a dangerous splendor, in trying to maintain his independent majesty. Masanissa has not made the same mistake. In the further development of the play, one of the dramatic questions will be whether he, too, will be attracted to the fatal error of opposing Rome, and an arcane historical "will," on behalf of personal good. Masanissa, however, returns to his original understanding of historical inevitability, as in the first scene, when he gives up his future love, Sophonisbe, and surrenders individual freedom and happiness for political power. There is no question of guilt as a flaw in character or as an ethical fault. In fact, twentieth-century readers are more likely to think of Masanissa as the sinner of the play, because of his betrayal of the queen. If the light and fire which dominate this drama visually indicate forces of consumption and immolation, if the factual "Flamme" and "Brand" which level Cyrtha have metaphorical counterparts in the "Flamme" and "Brunst" of passion, one must not think that Lohenstein "moralizes," as does Machiavellian Scipio. Syphax and Sophonisbe are not responsible for Cyrtha's fall morally; rather they are out of tune with history.

The Romans demonstrate what it means to be in tune with the march of things. Their self-conquest and rationality subserve ruthless ambition; they suppress the passions in favor of a single obsession: to rule. Especially in the case of *Sophonisbe,* the moral categories recede, and only the question of greatness in acting out a given role remains. Because the scales have tipped and she acts in opposition to overwhelming odds from the very start, our sympathy focuses on her. Masanissa speaks this important motif when he says: "The game is now reversed." ("Das Spiel ist itzt verkehrt" [I, 73].) In the world-wide contest between two major powers, reversal of fortune has taken effect. The astute Masanissa even thinks of opposition to Rome as a kind of madness, since it is marked with signs of victory by fate (I, 49–50). He already envisages Carthage crackling in flames. Lohenstein uses very effectively the audience's awareness of the story of Carthage's complete destruction in order to create the sense of fatefulness when Masanissa "predicts" so accurately. As in *Cleopatra*, the desire for freedom, the role of nobility, must stand against a tidal wave of destiny. Rome spreads out, encroaching upon the liberty of the world; it is "misfortune's sea," drowning and swamping all individuals and nations. Since human effort and thought cannot control its surge forward, Rome is associated with destiny itself (I, 82–84), as in Anthony's first speech.

Consciousness of this change in the game as a working of fate casts the loser into a tragic role, the role which Sophonisbe, too, finally accepts. Syphax already sees himself singled out by destiny as an example of man's helplessness and takes upon himself the plaintive role of fallen greatness, the prince cast down by "fortune's play" (I, 95–98). In the spectacle of history, fallen majesties offer the objects of pity for a seventeenth-century audience. Sophonisbe is more appealing than Syphax, of course, because of her resilient struggle against encroachment. She stays in the losing game tenaciously. Lohenstein himself documents his fascination with the metaphor of the world as a theater and with the concept of "play" *(Spiel)*, in its several senses as "game" and "drama," in his introductory poem to *Sophonisbe*. There he develops the basic conceits into a fantastic survey of the universe and man, whose "short time is nothing but a poem" (line 242). Also, distancing himself from the mad spectacle and observing it with sovereign wit, he implies that his own authorship is as sublime as that of the great world drama; for he says of his own playlet: "Ich liefer nur ein Spiel" (line 20). If this view of the "mad play of time" *(Agrippina)* is so clearly worked out, we can accept the sinful queens more as representative figures for mankind, as titanic as they are. And indeed, in the dedication to *Sophonisbe*, Lohenstein defines man as the "play of time." Speaking of the human role, its courageous uncertainty and indomitable restlessness, he says: "Für allen aber ist der Mensch ein Spiel der Zeit./Das Glücke spielt mit ihm/und er mit allen Sachen" (lines 73–74). In the three queenly histories, of Agrippina, Cleopatra, and Sophonisbe, an almost preconceived elegiac mood, a prejudicial sadness is invoked for those great roles which must terminate. Some unknown authorship is resolving and fixing them in the repertoire of the world theater. The intensity of the actor's playing becomes desperate, protest or resistance to the decreed conclusion, a pathetic self-assertion, and at last inevitable compliance according to the script.

Sophonisbe's personal story must be viewed not as Lohenstein's composition but, from his point of view, as what history dictated as subject matter for tragic interpretation. Lohenstein's laborious effort to annotate his play indicates his concern with factuality, history as the source of truth. One might go so far as to say, history is the author and Lohenstein, the often scorned polyhistorian, merely secretary. He has *authority* for presenting on stage the provocative, sometimes criminal, struggle of his women, whose charm no censure can obliterate. In his vision of time, greatness is the irreducible answer to the amorality of history; shorn of their distinctions, the remaining uniform characteristic of his heroines is their titanic attitude. Not the ethical substance of Epicharis' rebellion, but the greatness of her goal—to restore the lost nobility of the Romans—like the hopeless magnificence of her martyrdom, makes her a heroine. When Lohenstein creates the figure of Sophonisbe, she impresses us also because of her impossible aim of saving her fatherland, as Kayser convincingly states.[58] As in *Cleopatra*, so also in *Sophonisbe* the heroine is introduced in close association to the gods and cult of her doomed land; in fact, she is within the temple when first seen. Like Agrippina, she senses her

encirclement by danger and its tragic possibilities. Like Cleopatra, her great anxiety is not to be debased through a fall and
servitude. Like Epicharis, she would prefer the most gruesome
martyrdom (I, 226–30). After suspiciously spasmodic wavering
produced by the announcement of Syphax' capture, she decides
to accept her queenly identity with all the consequences of the
regal role. In keeping with the sacral atmosphere, she is ready
not only to undertake personal sacrifice, converting love for
her spouse into love of what he represents, the fatherland, but
also to offer up holy victims—her own children—to appease the
hungry deities: "Let my own blood bear witness/With what
milk of love I suckle my realm and people" (I, 359–60). This
manly hardness, readiness to kill her own offspring, assumption
of battle dress, reminds one of Epicharis' fanaticism, but strangely
united with an exotic personality.

The fervent self-immolation practiced in the state religion
and the suicidal tendency in the royal family, seen in the queen's
eagerness to sacrifice, characterize the Carthaginian civilization.
This body politic is represented by Sophonisbe, in whom conflicting extremes of passion—cunning, tenderness, hatred, and
savagery—contend (as the first chorus reiterates). She is associated with two warlike women: on the one hand, with the
fierce Amazon queen Penthesilea whom Kleist later portrays
with a divided, irrational nature; on the other hand, with Pallas,
the goddess of rationality, whose image, according to *Agrippina*,
chorus two, maintains empires, who is, therefore, the divinity
of *raison d'état*. Sophonisbe has this role as protectress of her
nation, but her actions are, in the final analysis, prompted by
fate. Amilcar's address draws together all the important terms
and indicates that the gods are only representative deities under
one anonymous power:

Die Rom für Afrikens Penthasilea schilt.
Schutz–Göttin unsers Reichs/ja Cyrthens Pallas–Bild!

Nun schöpf ich Lust und Muth! weil solch behertzt Entschlüssen
Muss vom Verhängnüsse/von unsern Göttern flüssen.

(I, 365–68)

So important is "feminine" nearness to fate that the queen has
her son Vermina dress in woman's clothes in order to pray to
the "gods." There is another motif from Lohenstein's drama as
a whole: if the gods are equated to fate, it is noteworthy that
in Sophonisbe's country they are gods of fire, devouring gods
who consume victims. When escaped Syphax suddenly reappears
and substitutes Roman captives for sacrifice, Sophonisbe in-
tuitively is doubtful whether the malevolence or favor (I, 446)
of the gods affects the proposed action. With pessimistic awe,
Vermina expresses the feeling that reason is incapable of illumi-
nating the mystery of fate; it sits on the judgment seat, inscrutable and depersonalized (I, 446–49). The Roman group, here
represented by the two victims substituted, curses the savagery
of human sacrifice. Roman reason condemns the barbaric in
Carthaginian civilization. When Lohenstein stages an actual
blood-sacrifice, he wishes to present evidence of the irrational
depths in a soul like Sophonisbe's, and one also sees the raging
of natural forces beneath the civilized mask, the sacred usages
of the falling kingdom.

One must not oversimplify the role of Sophonisbe as it
develops from the complicated traits revealed in the first act.
At first she bewilders the audience, the very effect she has on
her world; and in this resides a great part of her charm, for she
is distinctly the "light" in the play, upon whom focuses the look
of all who need release from the darkness of history. Her
appearance is often startling, as she takes risk after risk, assumes
costume after costume. To Syphax, she resembles a radiant angel
penetrating the dungeon to bring freedom (II, 251–53); this
unity of love and freedom is reminiscent of the sentimental
theme in *Ibrahim Bassa*. Love, prompting her generous rescue,

is an indomitable principle with chameleon-like disguises, of "Proteus' order" (II, 260–62). But Sophonisbe is fascinating because she obeys all the dictates of immediate necessity; these are irreconcilable. As a queen, she cannot avoid the reasoning of politics; as a noble, the commands of conscience. She must choose and act in crisis under political pressure. When she turns immediately from the accomplished freeing of Syphax to her plans for winning Masanissa, she is trying to control destiny through rationality and, like Cleopatra, hopes to use passion as a weapon (II, 307–8). She takes over the cause of the realm on an effective basis and believes that Syphax cannot rightly curse her, then, since she has broken his chains and is ensnaring Masanissa in her own for the good of their nation (II, 304 ff.). Motivated by love for her husband (Isabelle), by an impulse to liberate (Epicharis), by a desire to save her state (Cleopatra), she thinks that she is acting consistently and forgets, of course, that the game of passion is treacherous (Agrippina). Even though concerned with freeing herself, her spouse, her country, she is already playing her role too convincingly, drifting irresistibly. The queen is another variation, then, of an important figure, the deceived deceiver, in whom self-deception appears after a few scenes. Since Lohenstein loads his characters' statements with ironic hints, the audience views with apprehension her apparent fluctuation between loyalties, a bold maneuvering which she candidly "explains" as politics.

Masanissa experiences for a second time the shock of discovering Sophonisbe in radiant armor and after an impressive deed. Her loyal rescue sways him, for her influence as a liberating "light" still waxes, deceptively victorious, at this juncture in the play. As soon as he insists on personal rights to happiness (II, 411), and no longer subordinates his passions, his political judgment falters. Sophonisbe launches into an impassioned confession of her "flame" (II, 420); and he believes, under her spell, that he can outwit Rome by rushing into a *fait accompli,* an immediate marriage. Since recognition and maintenance of queenly identity are paramount conditions for her royal love, it remains to be seen just how far she has really committed herself in this seduction which suggests genuine attraction. Earlier, Masanissa has felt only the promptings of necessity, manipulated events, and adapted himself to destiny (I, 207); by joining the Romans, he has reversed in his own favor the fierce struggle for survival against Syphax. Behind the rhetoric with which he justifies expedient conduct is a brutal and melancholy fatalism; this sense Masanissa has dubbed the "sun of reason" (I, 212–13). His thoughts circle steadily the dilemma he recognizes and must resolve—a conflict between his ambition and his love for the queen, already inspired by the very first meeting. The identical image uttered so haughtily in the first line of the play returns with conscious irony: "Are you flinging yourself intentionally as moths do into the fire?" (II, 177). This internal discussion, another form of disputation, is carried on a stream of rhetoric. The principal terms of the rhetorical system remain "light" and "fire," which, as we already also know through our discussion of other plays, have contra-dictory implications. Masanissa feels himself divided, attracted by two opposed forces, the light of reason and the glow of Sophonisbe. Despite the argumentative exclamations, conjunctions, questions, one is conscious primarily of a mind in struggle and only secondarily of set patterns. Lohenstein evokes the emotions, capturing in Masanissa more the complexity of the man, in Syphax more the stereotype. Yet the monologue revelation of the Numidian's soul corresponds closely to the over-all picture of the world as something inconstant, shifting, reversing. That vision influences every aspect of the drama.

The question arises, perhaps, how far one should accept the statements couched in highly stylized speech as "genuine" expression of the dramatic persons. For example, in light of Sophonisbe's further behavior in this drama in which she seems

to reverse herself radically several times, first protesting love
for Syphax and next affirming love for Masanissa, one may be
tempted, if not yet familiar with the standard rhetorical appa-
ratus of Lohenstein's or his contemporaries' language, to associate the intricate verbal fencing only with her political and
dubious side, with the deceit and intrigue of court. Doubtlessly,
cunning goes with rhetoric, with artful speaking. Yet, even
though rhetorical formulas, abstract phrases, and conceits constitute an "artificial" mode of expression, one recognizes that
certain characters speak with a kind of honesty that shines
through the conventions, while devious intentions also stand out
sorely from pretended sentiments. The truth is that all persons
use the same "system" of speech, and that a listener distinguishes
character just as with any other conventional language. As in
the French classical theater, terms which sound so abstract to
the uninitiated reader actually carry powerful emotive force.
Such emblems form a network of possibilities of expression.
A definite language of "higher" souls, a distilled essence of
language, indicates adequately the movement of hearts.

Although both main characters share a common nature,
Lohenstein hints how deceptive the surface is, even prior to
showing what emerges from within. Sophonisbe's marital dress
gives her the resolute appearance of Roman "virtue"; in fact,
outwardly she disguises herself as a Roman soldier in order to
save her husband.[59] Yet inwardly she is the emotional queen
and attractive woman, in whom one hears weariness with the
world, desire to escape the debasement of captivity which
threatens her identity (II, 104–10, 115–16). This African
identity continually flares up in Masanissa, but eventually
becomes an exhausted mask. As one of Rome's agents for
enslaving Africa, he cannot also maintain temperamental or
real liberty. As Syphax says prophetically, Masanissa harbors
in his breast a "wolverine" which will devour his African nature
(II, 60–63). What this symbol of Rome means becomes clear

with the later appearance of Scipio, who eradicates the "deceptive" African triumph, just as he has mastered passions in himself. The opening scene of the third act shows Masanissa, like Anthony, opposed to his own advisers, who seek to dissuade him from a connection with Sophonisbe. They contend that the queen calculates politically for her homeland (III, 29). Sophonisbe infects him with the idea of "freedom," freedom for individual happiness, with its dangerous political possibility, a rupture with Rome (III, 41–42). The wedding ceremony, a lyric interlude, is the final triumph of Sophonisbe and likewise the play's optimistic peak. The solemnity and pomp of the cult create the atmosphere proper to the queen. On full stage, all present act as a chorus, operatically, to render the refrain after each ceremonial climax, invoking the grace of the victim-devouring fertility goddess Astarth for the marriage. Even this triumphal ceremony in the sacral sphere contains, as if beneath a deceptive mask, hints about the final power of "divine love" (Astarth) against the encroaching threat of Rome. The priest Bogudes prognosticates the couple's future; and as in *Cleopatra*, in which temple animals gave the signs, so here certain auguries, a heart that is too small and a flame that does not burn purely and brightly, cause foreboding.

The intrusion of realistic politics is swift, when Laelius and some Roman soldiers burst in upon the wedding and excite Masanissa by the threat to his bride's security. A quarrel over sovereignty flares up between the Roman officer and African king. He makes a hot and brilliant defense of Phoenician culture and goes so far as to raise himself the charge that Rome seeks to enslave the world (III, 192 f.). The climax of the African-Roman conflict in the third act comes when Laelius discovers the sacrifice of Roman victims and curses the practice of human immolation which so enrages Roman sensibilities. Yet, as Lohenstein sardonically demonstrates, Laelius' denunciation of savagery, idolatry, and inhumanity calls forth a bloody revenge.

The Roman wants to punish brutally the priest and others to expiate Roman blood. The author has no personal comment about the primitive forces unleashed for a "just" cause but stands aside, absorbed in the factuality of such gruesome behavior. Dramatically powerful is Bogudes' defense of his conduct as high priest. He rests his case on the mandate of sacred laws (III, 295), the same claim which all churches make; and Lohenstein, as author, does not invalidate or comment upon the assertion. Laelius calls this opinion mad (III, 296) and speaks of nature itself being revolted by human sacrifice (III, 305), only to proceed with a command that Bogudes be killed. Then Bogudes proclaims with great dignity his happiness in dying for the gods without having sullied himself. He has the triumphant and pathetic tone of a genuine martyr, yet he is a pagan, whose cult is barbarous:

> Solch Tod bestetigt es: Bogudes sey beliebt
> Den Göttern/denen er als Priester sich geweihet/
> Weil er zum Opfer selbst auf ihr Altar gedeyet;
> Ihr edles Creutze küsst.

> (III, 314–17)

Lohenstein even lends his speech the emotional appeal afforded by the supreme symbol of sacrificial death for Christians—the cross. This is a remarkable moment in seventeenth-century literature. After horrible human sacrifice there follows a passage in which the murderous priest justifies himself with a pathos based on the Christian tradition of piety, on language which a "humane" Laelius calls madness. Lohenstein rises above the conflict between two attitudes, the religious and the humanistic-rational, with cold examination of belief and action as *historical facts*. In the author's sphere of observation there exists no beautified truth, because the truth, as he sees it through history, can often be ugly. Bogudes' priesthood is horrid in many of its practices, spendid in its idealism, just as the Roman rationale is humane, ordered, legalistic, while Rome's program of conquest is brutal and bloody indeed. Lohenstein's superiority to dogmas and theories, lofty consideration of behavior without belief in the prejudiced notions of the actors, can be chilling and remind one of theatrical irony in Shakespeare's vein. Lohenstein bases the worth of his characters, not upon confessional grounds, but upon sheer greatness and appeal.

In this crisis Sophonisbe realizes that a breach will provoke disaster and does not want her new husband and protector to be threatened by Rome's wrath. Although her motive still is political, she may act already in part through love for Masanissa. Sophonisbe's readiness to perform on her countrymen the Roman act of revenge in return for her own personal and political survival gives us a shock similar to that which Queen Cléopâtre causes in Corneille's *Rodogune* (1644) by murdering her own son. Here, however, the Carthaginian queen again does not carry out her resolution, and one can admire her extreme purpose, yet need not regard her as an actual monster. A force which is ultimately to undermine her aims of state intervenes suddenly. Love, which Sophonisbe herself has said is protean (II, 260), intrudes in a new disguise. Syphax, the first prisoner among the North Africans, has been caught escaping in the dress of the hated Roman enemy. Recognizing his true identity, she trembles, powerless to strike. Lohenstein wants to magnify our horror only in order to build a surer foundation for our sympathy toward his heroine torn between her fierce political will and her heart. That organ which causes so much confusion for the queen apparently also disturbs her critics, who doubt not only the morality but the validity of her contradictory actions. Martin puts the case about as succinctly and negatively as possible: "Sophonisbe is first all heroine, then all whore."[60] But it is too easy to accept the view of Syphax himself, who wishes to kill her for what he imagines, as doubtless the audience has also momentarily accepted, to be dishonor and betrayal. Syphax is unable to alter his opinion, even though Sophonisbe, at her wedding to a rival king and at a time of personal danger, reaffirms her love for him, her captured spouse. Before questioning her sincerity, one must note that she fails to buy the confidence of Rome by a bloody act, although it might have worked in her favor permanently.

Precisely at the instant when she seeks to solidify her second marriage, the queen is compelled by chance to demonstrate loyalty to her first husband, even though her type of loyalty amounts to "madness." Although previously she may have imagined herself to be manipulating destiny, now she finds herself entangled in a hopeless contradiction with no way out. If the philosophy of power prompts her second marriage as a political arrangement, how easy then the consequential step ought to be. But Sophonisbe cannot kill the man she still loves and has never, in her own mind, deceived; fortune has divided them, she claims (III, 367). The vicissitudes of time do not, however, affect her love for him, which still pulsates in her breast (III, 371). By her adherence to her love for Syphax, Sophonisbe exhibits the traits of a tragically committed person rather than a manipulator of fortune. In answer to Syphax' question whether love can have a double seat in a pure heart, she replies with amoral candor that it has won a twofold place in her through necessity, and that *both* men are "true suns" to her (III, 375, 377). Sophonisbe has never in her own view acted unreasonably but only as a noble lover would wish her to do, since true love can deny nothing to the beloved (III, 390–95). She believes in her loyalty to both men! Without doubt Lohenstein has created a unique feminine personality and a heroine unknown in seventeenth-century drama; she clings irrationally to love and possesses simultaneously, in heart as well as fact, *two* husbands. As Kayser sees, Lohenstein is concerned not with a psychological problem of how one woman is drawn to two men, but with "the attested fact."[61]

In *Cleopatra* the imposing figure of Augustus comes on stage in the fourth act. The timing of this entrance relieves the anticlimactic drop which frequently plagues the interval between the third act, the turning point of a classicistic play, and the fifth act, its final resolution. Lessing, too, preferred introducing a fresh dramatic personality for the fourth act in his own play-wrighting. The suspense about Augustus runs as an undercurrent through the first three acts of *Cleopatra,* and he is the shadow over everything. His envoys and evidences of his intriguing mind enter and exit, as he remains spinning his net offstage. Scipio likewise has remained in the background and excited the audience's expectation. Now with his arrival a new and high concept of governing reason materializes before our eyes, dominates with confidence, the epitome of victory (IV, 38–40). Unmistakably, the machinery of the universe is geared in harmony with him. The word "drive" *(Trieb),* indicating a mechanistic view of natural law, occurs often after this moment, as in Masanissa's great monologue (scene four). The Roman Machiavellian knows all the levers and gears, may parade in the robes of historical "righteousness," that is, success. He has the poise, the convincing mask of greatness, a flawless role, in radical contrast to Syphax, who takes refuge from mortal judgment in the role of the defeated, an example of fallen nobility (IV, 53–57).

Scipio quickly decides about the queen—she is a political danger by virtue of her very existence. Because Scipio is not susceptible to inner conflict of passions, his speech is correspondingly clear and concise, razor-like. He must kill the beauty which seduces. The meeting with Masanissa is outwardly calm, open, and festive. There are only three speeches, Masanissa's tribute, Scipio's acceptance and bestowal of honors, and Masanissa's brief offering of a blessing. Yet the very smoothness

causes tension. The two leaders have carefully drawn a diplo-
matic veil before the court. Masanissa is rather extreme in
giving all to Scipio and demanding no war prize for himself,
a gesture to buy something costly. Scipio carefully avoids the
wrong indebtedness, publicly embraces Masanissa, and lauds
him with terms of fame, virtue, honor. Calling the African
brother and friend (IV, 177), he elevates him in public esteem
to the highest level. This gesture is the countermove, placing
Masanissa in an obligated position from which he can withdraw
only with difficulty. Scipio maneuvers to obviate any bargain
over the queen by returning into Masanissa's hands the crowns
and scepters. The intimate conference between the leaders further shows Scipio's mastery as a man of the world. The Roman
wants to lead the African toward self-control as the true heroism
and virtue, while the latter persists in a fatalistic belief that his
love is ordained, divine, therefore inconquerable. Scipio couples
scorn for heedless passion, "a blind drive" (IV, 247), with a
mandate, "master yourself" (IV, 259), patience with firm-
ness. His majestic poise allows, even demands, expression of
compassion, which is the luxury of his superior hold on life.
Behind the mask of the adroit statesman, the mentor expresses
personal care:

Er jammert mich/mein Freund; sein Leid geht mir zu Hertzen/
Ich hab Empfindligkeit und Theil an seinen Schmertzen/
Ich sorge für sein Heil.

(IV, 261–63)

This touch of the missionary fits well. As Lohenstein portrays
him, Scipio resembles a Jesuit-like ideal figure. He is a soldier,
realist about the world, given to absolute authority, ascetic and
puritanical in personal conduct, masterly in manipulating others
on behalf of power. One may believe in Scipio's compassion;

but then, one may also believe legitimately in the tears of a Counter-reformer who weeps before the stake on which a hopeless heretic perishes in error. The Roman's victorious optimism is aggressive even in the sphere of personal matters. Rome truly signifies the encroachment of political empire even upon personal freedom.

Scipio holds up to Masanissa the power ideal, power through the dominion of intellect; reason admits only a unified single passion—ambition. Thus reason, the instrument for ambition, kills the dangerous flesh. This ascetic doctrine brings forth what is perhaps Scipio's most sympathetic lines: "I am a man like you, but master of desires" (IV, 303). For a stoic, any involvement in the world, except for expression to truth, sullies. Scipio may appear to be moral, but in fact he is only puritanical for the sake of more effective involvement in history. Like Augustus, his hands are red with blood; the ethics of conquest permit him to put his crimes into a better light. In contrast, we hear Masanissa's bitter explanation: he is from Libya, where the sun and love glow more hotly in winter time than in Rome's summer, that northern midnight:

Ich bin aus Libyen. In unsern Städten blühet
Nichts/was nicht feurig ist. Die Sonn und Liebe glühet
Bey uns zur Winters–Zeit mit mehrer Krafft und Macht/
Als/wenn der Hunds–Stern brennt in eurer Mitter–Nacht.

(IV, 309–12)

His intense suffering on account of his very nature stirs compassion, and against this compassion admiration for Scipio wins little ground. Counter to Flemming's already cited choice of Gryphius' stoic martyr Papinianus, Nuglisch considers divided Masanissa not only as the greatest masculine figure achieved by Lohenstein but also as the supreme male character of "baroque" drama.[62] When Masanissa surrenders in tears to Scipio's demand, he is tormented by bad conscience on account of the oath he has given Sophonisbe (IV, 335–41), whereas Scipio dismisses even conscience with the coolness of "reason." Since in all of Lohenstein's plays, the love oath (moral freedom) is contrasted with oath-breaking (deception of trustless political life), Masanissa is driven not merely to lose his beloved but also his momentary inner security in his world. That is Lohenstein's vision of him as a victim of his own ambition and historical circumstances. The Roman or political clime is "midnight"; Africa gave "sun and light," being and love.

Masanissa's first thought in his monologue is of Sophonisbe, that she is to languish in Roman chains (IV, 345). He feels the full impact of tragic implications in his political character, asking: "Will not with her the light escape our eye?" (IV, 367). He vents his hatred of the Roman, whom he also fears, as hard, cruel, and ravenous; does not want to pay the price of the light of beauty, of personal happiness; and inveighs against the structure of the world, like a Christian frustrated by its darkness and disappointments, cursing empty wealth of greatness (IV, 380–85). One does not exaggerate by saying that Masanissa has, in knowing Sophonisbe, come in contact with a divine force; he still longs to have "Both virtue and form which in her are godly" (IV, 228). She incarnates the eternal charm of the universe. The second chorus of *Sophonisbe* proclaims love as the prime mover of the world and beauty as a manifestation of this force:

> Die Erd ist in den Himmel selbst verliebet/
> Sie schmückt im Frühling sich schön aus/
> Nur: dass sie ihm geschwängert Anmuth giebet.
>
> (II, 488–90)

Until line 400 of the fourth act, the turning point in the monologue, Masanissa acknowledges his dedication to the beautiful. As long as he is possessed with the idea of freedom, the yearning characteristic of Lohenstein's protagonists, he does not use the word "reason." But after this the other side of him, the political, resurges and he starts thinking in terms of the state and of reason. He tells himself: "The realm is your spouse" (IV, 406), words close to the final utterance of Corneille's Cléopâtre *(Rodogune)*, who has committed every crime against nature for power and dies, unlike Lady Macbeth, unrepentant. Masanissa sees a mechanistic or "Cartesian" universe, in which love is reduced to a base operation, a kind of enslavement in the physical system. Reason is extolled as the ideal, because it offers the possibility of manipulation, of "spiritual" direction. The metaphor of the clockworks (IV, 413–14) is wrapped in intensified Christian pessimism; the substitution of an anonymous mechanism (fate's) for a mysterious plan (God's) leads only to a worsened relationship between man's mind and his own human nature. Masanissa steels himself for betrayal of the queen with hollow moralistic rationalization (IV, 412–20).

The term "sober reason" (IV, 418–20) may impress one as a motto which belongs to a future age. In the eighteenth century it has emotional appeal as a slogan against that very courtly world of Machiavellian politics, which it here excuses. Clearly, one must not confuse this particular "sober reason" with the moral reason of the Enlightenment. Within the African plays, Masanissa forms the counter example to Anthony; within the total dramatic work, he stands in contrast to the earliest figure, Ibrahim Bassa. In the history of the German theater, he is the forerunner of the sobered, disenchanted prince, as in Hebbel's *Agnes Bernauer* or Grillparzer's *Jüdin von Toledo*. To be sure, the case for beauty is much stronger by the nineteenth century, and the modern prince can only accept the *fait accompli,* the sad fact of already perpetrated loss. Masanissa, however, comes from a literary period of religious frenzy. His thoughts are rich in violent contrasts and contradictions, which indicate a protagonist torn between poles of existence. Radically shifting from tender sorrow for Sophonisbe to bitter cursing of her, all his talk of reason cannot hide that he is a man of violent emotions. In his confused torments, his gesture of offering death is a strange final acknowledgment of love. For he wishes to keep his promise and save her from Roman chains, a token fulfillment of the pledge that signifies much to her. Although the final scene of the fourth act has shown the defeat of love by reason (IV, 457–58), although Masanissa has become an accomplice in her expected suicide, he imagines himself also in the role of redeemer. The powerful irrational theme of death the releaser comes forward on stage (IV, 481). Also, when the servant is to leave on his terrible mission and Masanissa falters, calls him back, sends him again, Lohenstein emphasizes that, despite his decision, the betrayer is more than a black villain.

The fourth chorus celebrates the "ethics" of absolute rule in an allegory of Hercules at the crossroads; the hero, in other words, faced by a test of inner fortitude. He must decide, as Masanissa just has, between bodily pleasure or voluptuousness (Wollust) and heroic rationality or virtue (Tugend). A tiny play in itself, with conflicting arguments and a resolution, this disputation's purpose is also social, to honor Leopold, who is naturally implied in the figure of Hercules. Virtue triumphs finally by unmasking pleasure on stage and revealing her as a hideous and loathsome creature. Pleasure is, then, the old "Frau Welt" figure in new variation. She represents the temporality of all earthly attractions, whose other side is disgusting decay and rot. The motif of stripping away the mask of outward appearance from the innerly nauseous deception has all the marks of Christian pessimism; this act of disenchantment resembles the Spanish moment of insight, or desengaño, when a beclouded hero sees through the nothingness of earthly attractions and reforms himself on behalf of spiritual goods. Here, however, not eternal salvation, but eternal honor and renown are to be won on the battleground of history (IV, 589–90). In direct praise of the emperor, Hercules judges the dispute. Tyrannic reason elevates a man above common humanity, indeed almost deifies him:

> Die Sternen werden seine Kron/
> Die Welt sein Reich/der Ruhm sein Thron.
>
> (IV, 601–2)

Hercules on the crossroads is a figure rather unappealing and cerebral next to provocative queen Sophonisbe or tormented Masanissa. In fact, one can question the lasting effect of the rational triumph in the fourth act and chorus. If there cool statecraft, power, and political success as the ultimate ends are celebrated over the beauty of earth itself, why then, one may ask, a fifth act at all? But Hercules' decision is not a final answer for the playwright. The play bears the name of a heroine as title, and it is she who comes back against all negative attitudes to dominate the stage. Since the more intellectual proofs about decadent North African culture and Sophonisbe's fate are given prior to the fifth act, the arrival of the inevitable comes at last as a relief. Emotional vents may be opened wide, and facts submerged in an ecstatic, rather than rational, moment. Death has been put off until the delayed anxiety creates almost a willingness on the part of the audience to submit to witnessing the end. In this sense, the fifth act becomes almost a play in itself, to which the preceding acts serve as preface. The plot of doom has led to the moment of physical exinction for some-one great, also for "something" great—a fallen empire. There-fore, the last act opens no longer upon a time for action in history but rather upon a grandiloquent pathos in answer to history. It is the moment of swansong. With this finality

Sophonisbe seeks out and is taken into the extratemporal, visionary sphere.

The temporal confines of the theater open for the irruption of eternity into the world. Lohenstein presents his equivalent of a religious "miracle" or a Greek godly intervention when Sophonisbe is initiated into the secrets of the future. Although Muris regards Dido's ghost only as a device, having nothing in common with the drama except the prior history of the showplace, Schaufelberger recognizes that some sort of penetration of the drama by an embracing system has occurred; Brede more accurately thinks of Sophonisbe's funeral dream as an "apotheosis."[63] Ordinary limitations of mortality are erased; indeed, she is immortalized as the figure representative of an epoch, and her death becomes the focal point where all ages converge. With the most radical step in his entire productivity, Lohenstein makes the queen timeless by allowing her to hear Dido, her ancestress, explain things to come, events which place even Rome, the rational monster and her destroyer, into a new perspective of historical limitation. Dido is a figure connected with Lohenstein's favorite mythology. Aeneas, fleeing burning Troy, is said to have brought with him some of the sacred fire from the fallen city, the fire which was then next transplanted to Rome and ensured Rome's life. Aeneas, according to Virgil, stopped first in Africa and became Dido's lover. But, following the dictates of the gods, who had chosen him for the heroic and political mission of founding Rome, he deserted Dido and left her to die through grief. Dido is now, in Sophonisbe's drama, associated with a special juncture of the heavenly luminaries and with special vision. Conditioned by suffering for contact with the sacred, Sophonisbe enters the temple with reverence and desire for these mysteries:

> ISt die das Heyligthum/in welchem von zwey Sternen
> Die blinden Sterblichen zukünfftge Dinge lernen.

(V, 1-2)

The response of Elagabal the priestess could almost belong to Masonic ritual. She speaks of clarification of the dark confusion of life, illumination of clouded thought, the enlightenment through knowledge:

Dist ist es. Weil ihr Aug auf Erden ales sieht/
So Tag und Nacht erhellt; ist auch ihr Geist bemüht
Den düsteren Verstand der Menschen zu verklären;
Denn die/die Wissenschaft des Künftigen begehren/
Auch Sonn und Mond hierumb andächtig ruffen an/
Erlangen irhen Wunsch.

(V, 3–8)

Behind this triumph of light lurks the notion of rebirth, a whole submerged reservoir of Christian emotions. Lohenstein, however, only approaches eighteenth-century feeling in the play *Ibrahim Bassa,* which more nearly satisfies the religious requirements, although it appeals for a cultural liberation and not conversion of infidels. Sophonisbe, the first play by Lohenstein to include a "miracle," if one discounts the poetic sea-rescue of *Agrippina,* exhibits ponderous and operatic pessimism. The somberness of the temple, the mystery of the cult do not give way to a limpid, humanitarian "explanation." If one were to pick a musical accompaniment for the fifth act, it would be Monteverdi rather than Mozart. Not the benevolent fate which brings together a Tamino and Pamina, but the cruel fate which sunders Dido from Aeneas, a historical fate reigns. There is no wise and controlling intellect of a Sorastro, but instead an ascetic, politic, cruelly realistic Scipio.

When Dido unfolds the course of Rome's climb, the era of servitude which it regards as "heavenly destiny" (V, 135), she reveals also that Rome will fall eventually through internal weakness and new conquerors and sketches the tides of history up to Lohenstein's day. This old Lohenstein trick, to "predict" certain things of which the audience is already aware as historical facts, gives an aura of inevitability to the vision. The deeds of the present, that is of Lohenstein's times, form her closing revelation. She sees in the seventeenth century the foreplay of still more heroic accomplishments to come, especially triumph over the Moslems. The crusade message of Isabella *(Ibrahim Bassa)* is heard in retrospect, from the mouth of an ancient heroine, as prophecy! Finished with a description of the "future," Dido again calls on Sophonisbe not to outlive Carthage's glory (V, 188). Knowing that Masanissa is unfaithful and that her country is forever doomed, Sophonisbe apostrophizes Africa in a plaint which shows how intimately her own soul is bound up with her land. Ready to follow Dido's pathway to fame, she wants to offer up herself and the city in a gigantic funeral pyre. She knows that no enemy can dishonor the dust. Her decision calls forth a beautiful speech in which the ecstasy of self-immolation immediately strikes one's attention. This speech is at the same time a defense of all that she stands for. The core of the best Lohensteinian tragedy is expressed in these words which smack of neo-Platonic mystique:

Die Flammen/die uns fassen/
Muss jeder Mensch verehrn/der Gott ein Opffer bringt.
Sie sind die Flügel auch/durch die die Seele schwingt
Sich zum Gestirn empor. Durchs Feuers Kräffte werden
Beseelet Erd und Meer. Die Glutt vertritt auf Erden
Der Sonne Gütt und Ampt; sie ist ihr Göttlich Bild.
Kein Thier als nur der Mensch braucht Feuer; denn es kwillt
Sein Wesen vom Gestirn. Es reinigt/was beflecket/
Es ist der Welt ihr Geist/das alle Sachen hecket/
Der Anfang/in den sich auch alles äschert ein.
Welch ein gelücklich Grab wird uns die Glutt nun sein:
Eilt diesemnach/ und reisst die Fackeln vom Altare/

Steckt Burg und Tempel an. Mehr als beglückte Baare!
Wo Reich und Königin den Staub zusammen mischt/
Und ihr verspritztes Blutt auf frischen Bränden zischt!

(V, 226–40)

First it is necessary to accept all terms both as emblems and as images. Quite literally, the historical situation is one of conflagration and the razing of a city. Sophonisbe's intent is equally literal, to immolate herself. Yet the "flames" she refers to are also metaphoric for her loves, or love per se. Love is her fate; its seizure is fate's power in exercise. Sophonisbe believes that any person with true piety will feel and honor her downfall; the reaction she expects is a religious awe toward the spectacle she provides, as an example of a fated queen. Consciousness of destiny inspires a new form of worship, respect for the dead and for monuments as at the end of *Cleopatra*. These may be of individuals or cities or empires, in artworks or in memory. What then does it mean, if the "flames" are further "wings"? The expression of ascension rings very Christian, but here has to do with a *worldly* flight to the stars. This flight is both release of the soul and a kind of apotheosis. On the one hand, Sophonisbe may be saying something simple: that love lifts the soul heavenward, blissfully. On the other hand, she can also mean that her love has precipitated her fall but led her onto the pathway of immortalizing death.

She expresses the belief that love is the motivating force of the universe, the prime mover (see the second chorus). It is the earthly representation of the sun's action, and thus divine. Everywhere the literal parallel, fire and light, is sustained. The significant indication of her double meaning is the statement that no animal but man needs fire because his being originates from the stars. She elevates love, very distinctly differing from the play's Roman view, to a stature above animal nature; she connects man's special nature with love itself, the mover of the whole universe. One must here think of love as the earthly aspect of a principle permeating everything, a godly principle like the ether or fire of pre-Socratic philosophy. But no beneficent principle is meant; the traditional image of purification by fire implies tragedy. The sidereal origin points to the fiery consumption of man; he returns to his origin in the form of burnt-out ashes, cosmic dust. Sophonisbe's astral image is well taken, for a queen must aspire to the stars. They are symbols of awesome majesty, fixed, eternal. And from this consideration she rushes into mad self-destruction, yearning for fixation in the freedom of the grave, calls to her people to take torches from the altar, a holy source, and set on fire the city and temple, so that she and the realm may mix their ashes.

This touch of berserk love for her homeland makes a powerful impression. She thinks she must save the holy places from Roman desecration, especially the sun's, from whom she (like Phèdre) is descended. At this moment, the heartsick messenger arrives with the poison. Sophonisbe accepts the drink with joy, in fact, as a token of love:

> Willkommen süsser Tranck! Ich nehm ihn freudig an/
> Weil Masanissa mir nichts bessers schencken kann.
>
> (V, 307–8)

Despite the bitter tone of the word "bessers," her mind is already set on such a liberation, the "wished-for draught of freedom, desired marriage gift" (V, 309). Sophonisbe does not fall a fraction of an inch out of her role, a role which began as "acting" in necessity, and is now her true self. In her final moments of life she does not tear away a mask and show a Sophonisbe, let us say, prior to contact with Masanissa; instead she uses the opportunity to bless him and reaffirm her affection:

> Es lebe Masaniss/und dencke dieser wol;
> Die ihn itzt sterbende zu gutter Nacht gesegnet.

Geh meld ihm: dass uns dis/was uns von ihm begegnet/
Den Leib trennt/nicht die Lieb. . . .

(V, 316–19)

She asks forgiveness for her weakness in having married two
men, because fate pressed her, but never denies or withdraws
her love. In other words, the heroine maintains the unusual
position of having two husbands to the end, and beyond.[64]

Lohenstein does not make her conform to a confessional
model, to a paper existence. She cannot stop being herself.
Therefore, she confesses double affection at her wedding to
Masanissa, surely the wrong time for such a declaration by a
deceiver, and also at the time of her death, when she no
longer needs to deceive anyone. It is of interest to return to
the originator of most negative interpretations of Sophonisbe's
character. In *Critische Betrachtungen über die poetischen
Gemählde der Dichter,* analyzing the queen "without morals
and character," Bodmer is too perceptive to overlook the fact
that Sophonisbe continues to love illicitly, while ruing her
misdeeds, or to fear for her personal freedom, while acting as
a devoted mother of her country and family, etc.; but he is
incensed over her persistent unheroic heroics, that is, over
her resolute assertion of "contradictions."[65] Perceiving what
Sophonisbe does in fact do, Bodmer disallows it as deviationism
from his ideal of unified character, i.e., moral harmony. Later
critics sometimes unfortunately forget even *what* the queen
maintains to her end. Sophonisbe's language emphasizes Christian sentiments such as sacrifice and forgiveness, but on behalf
of her sinful attachments, actions for the good of more than
one husband. Isolated and deprived even of the comforting
memory of a spouse so good and blind as Anthony, she achieves
added stature in her loneliness as a victim of ingratitude. This
she enhances by a willing exit, which can help Masanissa and
prove her own magnanimity. In Lohenstein's drama, magna-

138

nimity is associated with purity *(Ibrahim Bassa, Epicharis)*,
and thus Sophonisbe attains a kind of purification.

This other high and noble side of Sophonisbe is also stressed
through her sharpened *vision* in unmasking death's terrors.
Such awareness marks her as a "purified" heroine, although
Lohenstein has never made her take back one iota of her illicit
dual passions! In her own thoughts she is far beyond earthly
imprisonment:

> Vertrautste/nunmehr ist der güldne Tag erschienen/
> Des Glücks/der Eitelkeit/der tausend Seelen dienen/
> Ihr Joch zu werffen ab; die Larve wegzuzihn
> Gespenstern/die mit nichts sich uns zu schrecken mühn.
> Der Todes–Schatten schafft nur blöden Augen Schrecken.
>
> (V, 325–29)

Sophonisbe's death agony is majestic further because her concern
concentrates on others and she thinks, as a queen and mother,
of her subjects' welfare.[66] Her wish is that her death could buy
their happiness, redeem them from Rome, but her sorrow is the
knowledge of the inevitable. Thus she turns entirely to death
for final consolation: "Elisa calls to me that I was born free"
(V, 429). With great ceremony she has distributed her royal
jewels and called especial attention to her earrings, symbols of
nobility (V, 424) and divine connection (V, 421). This recalls
the moment in *Cleopatra*, when Augustus takes the dead queen's
earrings as a sacred token for the shrine of Venus in Rome.
Masanissa arrives in desperation: "I murderer!" (V, 519). He
is about to expiate his crime when Scipio arrives. But, then,
Masanissa's punishment is that he must continue to live.

As soon as the Roman enters, a new personality rules.
Masanissa's brain is said to be enveloped by a "dream," his
heart by "desire," while "reason" will chase away these clouds

(V, 572–74). Scipio reduces Sophonisbe's double love, just witnessed sympathetically, to lasciviousness and faithlessness. However, the prestige of Scipio is not strong enough to dispel the lasting effect of the funereal scene for the audience. The fifth act stands out as a "separate drama," dedicated almost exclusively to her suicide, with scarcely any progress in plot action. The finale resembles the close of Gryphius' *Papinian*, in which a related retardation and attention to death occurs. A comparison of the *Cleopatra* of 1661 and the *Cleopatra* of 1680 also shows that the expansion of the fifth act into a "play in itself" is an artistic principle which Lohenstein shares with his contemporaries.[67] With Sophonisbe dead, the discrepancy between the mandate of reason and the appeal of beauty and greatness is sensed deeply. The irreconcilable division in the soul of Masanissa makes him rather than Scipio into the ultimate picture of humanity and, although not an ideal model like Scipio, doubtlessly the focus of our tragic awareness and our sympathy. The fallen king Syphax is all hatred and dejection; the Roman leader all poise, rationality, superiority. But Masanissa is the tragically purged and affected king who has lost his one happiness and pitifully submits to politics. Life, with its unreasonable reasons, love and beauty, is dead; Masanissa will labor now to "conquer himself":

> Ich wil/Grossmächtger Held/mich mühn zu überwinden;
> Wo meine Wunden nur noch Salb und Pflaster finden;
> Weil doch mein halbes Hertz in ihr begraben liegt;
> Jedoch/da Sie und Ich nicht diese Gnade krigt:
> Dass ihre Leiche nicht wird erst nach Rom geschicket/
> Da ihr Begräbnüs ihr von Römern wird verstricket/
> Mag ich lebendig nicht solch Hertzeleid schaun an.
>
> (V, 585–91)

Despite Scipio, Masanissa still acknowledges his debt to Sophonisbe and will keep his promise, paying last respects and performing the burial office for her, much as Cleopatra did for Anthony. Such a request Scipio cannot refuse. Then the first step in fulfilment of the prophecy: he gives the order that, as an example to the world, Carthage be reduced to ashes.

Many traits of this final scene call to mind Hebbel's drama, and especially *Agnes Bernauer*. The beauty of woman is dangerous in life, honored in death. The older and tried statesman Scipio is forced to kill Sophonisbe because he understands only history as his law; the subordinate ruler must suffer and accept his loss, emerging sobered from the "dream" of life into a political carer. The emphasis on a historical process which insists on victims is very similar, despite the wide separation of the authors in other respects. Lohenstein has a last line, a shout by all on stage, to affirm the hierarchical principle of the state or historical process over the individual: "Dass Rom und Scipio und Masanissa blühen" (V, 618). The order is striking; the *vivat* goes from the superindividual entity, "Rome," to the almost superhuman hero of history, "Scipio," whose added name "Africanus" really identifies him as a concept rather than creature, and finally to Masanissa, the weaker king and man.

As in *Cleopatra*, the final chorus establishes the ultimate context for the play. Fate discourses with four great monarchies or empires, the Assyrian, Persian, Greek, and Roman. Although the doctrine of the Holy Roman Empire of the German nation is celebrated as ordained and the play ends in homage to the ruling house of Austria, this is said without reference to the Christian God. Rather, fate—operating behind the veil of history—appoints and distributes the rights. As its personification says, there is an invisible law ruling history: grandeur cannot endure; the great realms of this world flourish and fade—

> IHr grossen Reiche dieser Welt/
> Die ihr verblüht seyd/und solt blühen.
>
> (V, 619–20)

Fate invites competition for the victor's crown, which goes to the strongest (V, 630). In such a context, beauty indeed seems almost a gratuitous and tragic phenomenon; inexpedient loyalty a gesture in protest against the universe itself. We should understand that fate's speech is an attempt by Lohenstein to formulate natural law on the highest level of abstraction. But, of course, here nature encompasses more than the limited garden of moral existence. He is not glorifying might as right or advocating historical determinism; he is defining the hard facts as he has seen them, through a completely depersonalized voice. We know full well, from reading the African plays, that Lohenstein dwells upon what is mysteriously gratuitous: beauty, feeling, and other manifestations of man as a creature not in tune with the iron law. He is fascinated by any area of resistance to necessity, because struggle ennobles man. However, on the arcane level of fate, far above the turmoil of history, Lohenstein allows the particular drama, which in human eyes looms so large, to fade away into the universal vision, where whole civilizations rather than individuals play roles as ascendant and declining actors. In his view, nevertheless, the microcosmic and macrocosmic are interlocked; we merely shift our attention to an example, when we observe the throes of a falling potentate whose own being is identified with that of his nation.

The dream of absoluteness, of final golden tyranny, suddenly seems to negate all that Lohenstein has spoken previously through the personification "fate." After judging successive empires, it decides that Germany will inherit permanent control of the world. But this arbitrary freezing of the effectiveness of the iron law of collapse is, after all, whether flattering propaganda or ardent wish, a conscious, resolving negation. For Lohenstein to accept an endless process of life caught in the unredeemed necessity of failure, he would only have to omit the utopian leap of faith. To be sure, his faith is a kind of Renaissance vision—a hope based on great expectations, not on the documented past as he knows it, a melancholy record of debacles and heroic gestures. The three old continents, Europe, Asia, and Africa, therefore welcome the newest continent, America, into the world picture. The prospect of a "new world" which so excited European thought is incorporated into Lohenstein's scheme of history. A different "eternity" must be substituted for fate's older iron law. He is able, using the fabulous expanse of the still undiscovered and of the newly discovered, to present the dream of the *endlessness* of Austria's happy rule. To modern readers it may appear odd that a play which shows a queen's inevitable fall through destiny also is used to celebrate eternal power for one house. But the contrast between the implied grandeur of the glorified patrons and the timely bondage of the play's subjects is hereby all the more striking. It is hard to believe that Lohenstein did not really see beyond his choruses which celebrate German rule, when he saw so clearly the life cycle of empires in analogy to man's. Yet his novel *Arminius,* the last great project of his own life, indicates otherwise. Like so many of his age, Lohenstein was at home in a mystically tainted "interpretation" of the cosmos. He may well have *believed* in a special destiny for the Germans. This hope caused him to indulge in many absurdities which contrast sharply with the harsh realism of his drama. One needs only point out the traces of this belief in his African tragedies and their final shape, a mythology of German primacy, as in the "aria of Queen Germany" (*Arminius,* II, 446). Against the operation of destiny, against the prestige of past history, his fertile mind constructed a gigantic reinterpretation of history, the story of Germany, the "exception."

If Lohenstein will be remembered, however, it shall not be on account of the "exception" to his own picture of history, but rather for his plays. Lohenstein's arcane "fate" changes theater from an edifying spectacle into the showplace of mysterious purgation. His terrifying dramas of defeat keep alive the concept of a titanic form of being, buttressed no longer by a dogma of salvation or by a rigid doctrine of rationality, but rather by an elusive notion of freedom. Lohenstein became the great secular dramatist of the seventeenth century in the German tongue by expressing this anxious aspiration to be liberated.

Chapter Seven

THE DRAMATIC SPECTRUM

IT IS FITTING to close our discussion of Lohenstein's drama with his best work, *Sophonisbe*. The play derives ultimately from the Renaissance attempt to restore ancient tragedy, which began with the first regularized imitation of classical rules in Italian, the *Sophonisba* (1529) of Giangiorgio Trissino (1478–1550). But it comes also at the end of a long development and during the transition to "modern theater" marked by Racine's humanized classicism. As Fritz Strich and others have pointed out, the golden age of the theater really started, however, not in the Renaissance but in the baroque period.[68] Lohenstein represents, therefore, a late dramatist writing after the peak of change and on the downslope. The pathways of transmission from Italy, large areas of which were ruled by Spain, to France, England, and the rest of Europe and, likewise, the influences which accompanied the revived tragedy at various stages have been explained frequently. One key factor for Germany was the spread of "Spanish" influence by the Jesuit theater during the important period (end of the sixteenth century) when the theater itself was becoming the great metaphor of existence. Of course, many titles such as Corneille's *Cid* or Kyd's *Spanish Tragedy* bear witness outside Germany to the importance of Spain at the height of her power, in addition to Italy. With the early sweep of the Renaissance through France in the sixteenth century, the imported "théâtre des Italiens" flourished; and the first French tragedy, regulated like Trissino's after the precepts of the ancients, soon appeared, namely the *Cléopâtre* (1552) of Etienne Jodelle (1532–73). The flood of Sophonisbes and

Cleopatras thereafter in both France and England was enormous.[69] In the former land, a unified national classicism was established, and the available models largely determined its theatrical expression, while the English participated more freely. Even as late a writer as Thomson—so important for the German eighteenth century because of his interest in "nature"—paid tribute to the Carthaginian queen in the Prologue to his own *Sophonisba* (1730); he saw the first Italian tragedy as a historical beacon on the edge of the Dark Ages—

> When Learning, after the long *Gothic* night,
> Fair o'er the Western world renew'd his light,
> With arts arising *Sophonisba* rose.

Needless to say, Thomson here spoke sentiments not as palatable to the German nation during its own floration; it became oblivious to the whole picture of humanistic tragedy. The Germans had suffered long from a sense of inferiority in regard to the populous, centralized, dominant French, and found it convenient to identify with the English during the latters' Augustan age (after the Glorious Revolution, 1688). Thus the sentimental critics could enjoy Milton, a rhetorical poet *par excellence,* but frown upon the bombastic French, or accept Lady Macbeth, but not Corneille's Cléopâtre *(Rodogune)*. The German Romantics, though avidly searching the past, tended to react favorably only to whatever in the Renaissance did not come too directly through the French. They continued the interest of the Storm–and–Stress movement in the Elizabethans and rediscovered a contemporary of Gryphius, Pedro Calderón de la Barca (1600–1681), whose world theater of theodicy struck many familiar chords. Although the plays of Christopher Marlowe (1563–93) exhibited bombastic traits from Senecan theater and fascination with Machiavellian concepts, these seemed more acceptable, because from the pristine age of

Shakespeare (1564–1616), than did the works of John Dryden (1631–1700), who was under the influence of French classicism in its late, pruned phase.[70] In short, just as the French were long blind to Shakespeare's greatness, so the Germans failed or refused to comprehend Corneille. Such cultural bias is quite normal; for example, in America the tendency has been subservience to naturalistic theater, as modified by Freudian psychology, resistance to newer trends like expressionist drama, and a limited concept of Greek tragedy as "Sophoclean."

The purpose here is not to belittle, but rather to recognize, predilections. It would be a gross lapse of judgment to assign to Lohenstein any but a modest place in the Age of the Theater solely on the grounds that he has been neglected and misunderstood. One needs only mention a few names from that age in order to realize that Lohenstein must be measured against giants. But if we think of the development of Renaissance neo-classical theater, arising in Italy under the influence of Senecan dramaturgy and the Machiavellian re-examination of humanity, we can better comprehend his strange blending of ancient heroism, stoic dignity, and pessimistic spite with the religious yearning and erotic nihilism of the late seventeenth century. The context of his message is no more foreign to the message than is our twentieth-century context. Yet since that message provides the only unity between our distinct times, the context is a serious problem. The fact is that today scarcely a German actor can read Lohenstein correctly, while the extravagances of much of Elizabethan diction appear familiar. Before the German alexandrine line was perfected and raised to a level comparable to the French, it went into rapid decline. And the historically untenable doctrine of "natural" rhythms suited for German and English theater still inhibits confident interpretation.[71] To catch the unfamiliar accents, one must virtually rush to and fro between the Old Vic' and the Comédie Française. Lohenstein was affected by the currents of Elizabethan naturalism and Renaissance curiosity, but also by the stately heroics of the French stage, with its almost exclusively regal characters. Thus an actor trained in the tradition delimited by Lessing would find it difficult to feel at home in roles showing some luster, because he could not associate easily with the "French" element in them. Certainly the sententious language of Lohenstein is a barrier, because it belongs to no understandable style of acting prevalent in German lands, except perhaps older operas, but these are carried by their music more than their language.[72] The declamatory style which is preserved, doubtlessly rather pure, on the French classical stage offers many hints—but German theater is in contact with the English, not the French, seventeenth century.[73]

Recognizing this situation, we must not be hasty in judging Lohenstein's dramatic works as a whole. The stylistic traits of the seventeenth century in Germany, as distinct from its poetics, are yet to be established with the same critical thoroughness and control exercised in the examination of periods like romanticism, classicism, etc. Most commentators agree, nevertheless, that Lohenstein—were his language treated thoroughly—would remain an example of what French theorists designate as *galimatias* or *phébus*; his metaphors go to the limits of the possible for his time.[74] His attempt to elevate poetic diction above prose contributed generally to the eighteenth-century stock of dramatic expression, as well as specially to the bases for pathetic speech (Haller, Klopstock, Schiller). But perhaps more importantly, Lohenstein represents one of the last German poets who, like his Romance models, preserved the connection with late antiquity. Racine, with his purified drama, religious pessimism, and sentimental strain, and Lohenstein, with his freedom from the strict conventions, his historicism, and uncouth naturalism, both were steeped in *authorities,* the ancient classics. We must concede that, subject to modifying influences, these authorities formed a spiritual reference not always congruent with

Christian traditions. The revival of tragedy in the golden age
of the theater may well reflect the great crisis of the Christian
world at the time of the wars of religion and the birth of
modern science. Lohenstein's message hovers between cynical
rationalism and heroism; his hyperbolic speech can sink platitudinously or soar hysterically. But if he is pitched always a
bit high, this may be a sign of his particular tendency not to
portray varied situations of life but to put almost unanswerable
questions about destiny in the heat of struggle. His plays all
present situations of desperation and, therefore, may translate
into secular terms the religious anxiety generated by a century
of normalized catastrophe. They also demonstrate concern with
the limiting of special, even exotic, forms of being; it is as if,
were we to pick any central theme, Lohenstein writes about
titanic character, that proves itself and its reality in resistance
to a threat which is inherently opposed to such uniqueness. In
this sense, then, he combines the *vanitas* motif with an older
concept of the hero as demigod.

Whether through Isabelle's urge to flee the absolute enslavement of Turkey, Epicharis' struggle for republican freedom
against imperial tyranny, Agrippina's attempt to save herself
from monstrous threats, or Cleopatra's and Sophonisbe's resistance to the encroachment of Rome upon their independent
realms, Lohenstein expressed an impulse for freedom. The roots
of the inspiration were in Christian stoicism, the same soil
which nourished Gryphius. And hence also the irrational tendency evident in glorification of suffering and in suicidal defiance
of overwhelming threat. Lohenstein explored three secular possibilities: first, the original, sentimental equation of love, death,
and freedom, expounded through martyrs not sullied by the
slightest taint of ambiguous involvement *(I. B.);* next, the
political martyrdom of a fanatical heroine forced to use the
instruments of a corrupt world in the fight to reform it, against
the decree of Fate *(Ep.);* and the catastrophe of anti-heroical

greatness, the example of a fascinating sinner trapped by her human condition *(Ag.)*. The confrontation of civilizations, or of historical forces on a vast scale, was suggested in the first Turkish play. One Roman play showed the noble futility of combatting the "Turkish" epoch, the iron age of slavery in all its aspects, represented by the Roman Empire and corrupt courtly, political man *(Ep.)*. The other Roman play exhibited criminality in the context of historical doom and also indicated an all-pervading theory that man's involvement in history was a universal tragic process *(Ag.)*. Lohenstein used the story of the fall of Troy rather traditionally as a myth for the collapse of a civilization (Rubria chorus). Intertwining the standard metaphors for love or passion with the image of sacred fire, i.e., the life force of a whole people, he explained destructive trends in terms of waning moral vitality.

Each drama was excerpted from a gigantic, awesome, and inexorable process. Caught in any microcosmic moment in this shifting of vital forces, hero and anti-hero were subordinate. Although noble protagonists still referred to higher standards, to permanent justifications beyond their limited human condition *(I. B., Ep.)*, another elusive, non-rational measure of stature seemed available to actors strutting and fretting before extinction *(Ag.)*. Whereas Ibrahim, Isabelle, Epicharis, and Seneca invoked solid moral claims beyond the sphere of power, Agrippina made her impression solely through desperate manipulation. But the criminal had to be magnificent, and then exposed as a creature subject to human misery, before she acquired any tragic coloration. Her struggle against invincible doom finally put her into the category of victim, guilty but utterly abject; however, what was more important, her erotic beauty, now fading and condemned to obliteration, was glorified as an indication of divine origin, even greatness of spirit (shipwreck chorus). This neo-Platonic emphasis of the enigmatical function of beauty, but also of its divine origin, was present in all the plays to some extent. In *Ibrahim Sultan,* Lohenstein did not simply revert to his original perspective and endow a pure heroine with beauty that corroborated her sublimity; she was also the instrument of an inscrutable, recondite authority—fate. While critics have stressed obvious contrasts of positive and negative, such as that between reason and passion or the characters of Ambre and the sultan, etc., they have neglected Lohenstein's esoteric tendencies, a seventeenth-century penchant for occult perceptions. In *Agrippina,* he hinted at an impenetrable mystery by portraying anti-heroic attractiveness. Nor did he return to the safe moorings of an unambiguous dichotomy in the second Turkish drama, but pessimistically plumbed unfathomable depths—the human psyche, the ocean never to be explored satisfactorily (*I. S.,* IV, 263–67).

Cleopatra was a yet more complicated protagonist; victimizer and deceiver, also unwitting instrument of fate, she provoked sympathy through her intensely blind struggle to maintain an entire realm. Despite all her craft, she could not obviate disaster. Cleopatra chose to rescue her nobility, a high form of freedom based on regal dignity and power, by exiting from dangerous entanglement. This extreme answer, this insistence on role or freedom, made no reference to a moral judgment as in *Ibrahim Bassa,* and the stature of the claimant rested only on evidences of titanic will and exceptional charm. While Agrippina was assassinated—thus victimized in order to acquire the character of a "guilty martyr"—Cleopatra killed herself like the political idealist Epicharis, in order to maintain greatness by a supreme, fixating gesture. Her suicide was by far more imposing because it led to a final development of character and insight into the tragic futility of her role. She reaffirmed her inner connection to the lost bliss represented by Anthony. The love-death, with nihilistic tones of a redemption foreshadowed in *Ibrahim Bassa,* evoked the melancholy of wasted life in the corrupt human condition. The extratemporal realm of love returned with slight moralizing rationale; tribute was paid to a wish-dream of an earth where mankind could live in natural joy (chorus four). Lohenstein most successfully enriched his concept of the criminal heroine with Sophonisbe's strange and unreasonable candor. All the absolute positions were erased. Sophonisbe was torn by passions but inspired by the high goal of serving her country, bigamous but loyal to those whom she loved (I. B.). Not a Cleopatra by any means but rather a victim committed by love from the start, she was, nevertheless, like Cleopatra, the high, queenly sacrifice of a civilization in its death agony.

What really distinguished Sophonisbe, however, was that she experienced a vision of world history. This made her a companion of those ancient "saints" who through sheer suffering gain insight into the universe or are taken up by the gods. Cleopatra's ultimate realization of the beauty of Anthony's love was bittersweet bliss. In Sophonisbe, the sinner and victim, no outer example, only inner dedication, was a final guide. She transgressed, but her excessive loves, clearly against reason though ostensibly undertaken for distinct aims, were a "tragic flaw." Although the term from Shakespearean criticism is not precise, one must note that Lohenstein developed the stoic martyr drama, once in the shadow of Christian beliefs and rationalistic philosophy, into a tragedy of his own. Despite all moralizing to the contrary, only love suggested any final picture of the state of permanence vainly desired. The contrasting grim reality of political glory—amoral and cold monumentality—only made the failure more agonized. In Lohenstein's African plays, man became tragic by his own gesture and was not elevated by any external redemption. His meaning was contained implicit in the mysterious script of the world-theater, in which he was a self-conscious actor. Sophonisbe, suffering, was the first heroine who very clearly rose above the script and read it—broke the chains of temporality.

Of course, that apotheosis is a penetration of temporality by some supernatural meaning, and in this regard related to the Greek *deus ex machina,* such as the rescue of Euripides' Medea in a chariot drawn by dragons, or to the Christian miracle, such as the sudden opening of the stage in seventeenth-century theater for divine intervention, illumination, transfiguration, etc. But both of the latter salvations are attempts to evade tragedy, to explain it away, whereas Sophonisbe's vision is purely insight into, not avoidance of, real defeat. As remote as her play is from that of Oedipus at Colonnus, Sophonisbe's suffering is consummated in a sacred place; we witness this, whereas the profounder cult experience in the grove of the furies is reported by Theseus. In its simplest terms, Lohenstein's drama is an attempt to state the limitation of man as a law, but not an explanation; our experience of the story of defeat is the real pathway to understanding this human condition.

Notes

NOTES

Chapter One

1. References to the plays will be by act (Roman numerals) and line (Arabic numerals) in the critical editions prepared by Klaus Günther Just, *Türkische Trauerspiele, Römische Trauerspiele*, and *Afrikanische Trauerspiele* ("Bibliothek des Literarischen Vereins in Stuttgart," Nos. 292–94 [Stuttgart, 1953–57]). Whenever needed for clarity, a title will also be cited in abbreviation (*I. B., I. S., Ep., Ag., Cl., So.*). For bibliographical aid, consult Just's edition; and Hans von Müller, "Bibliographie der Schriften Lohensteins." *Werden und Wirken: Festgruss für K. W. Hiersemann* (Leipzig, 1924).

2. For treatments of *Arminius*, see Louise Laporte, *Lohensteins Arminius* ("Germanistiche Studien," Vol. XLVIII [Berlin, 1927]), and Max Wehrli, *Das barocke Geschichtsbild in Lohensteins Arminius* ("Wege zur Dichtung," Vol. XXXI [1938]).

3. Lohenstein is available in older collections, such as the reprinted Neukirch anthology, *Herrn von Hoffmannswaldau und anderer Deutschen auserlesener und bissher ungedruckter Gedichte, erster Theil* ("Neudrucke," N.F. 1 [Tübingen, 1961]), and in several newer anthologies, such as Max Wehrli's *Deutsche Barocklyrik* (Basel, 1945). Fellgibel, Lohenstein's original publisher, put out (Breslau, 1680) the most complete selection of poems, along with diverse short prose pieces and the plays *Cleopatra* and *Sophonisbe*, in what is known as "Collection A 1"; I cite from the section "Himmel–Schlüssel," p. 36. Unfortunately, I have not yet been able to obtain Helmut Müller's "Studien über die Lyrik D. C.s von Lohenstein" (dissertation, Greifswald, 1921).

4. In "Collection A 1," section entitled "Rosen," p. 116 ff.

5. Concerning the hegemony of politics in the drama, see Willi Flemming, "Das deutsche Barockdrama und die Politik," *Euphorion*, Vol. XXXVII (1936).

6. *Geschichte der deutschen Poetik* (Berlin, 1958), I, 41. In addition to Markwardt's excellent treatment of the period, see Paul Böckmann, *Formgeschichte der deutschen Dichtung* (Hamburg, 1949), Vol. I, chap. iv, on the *elegantia* ideal and rhetorical pathos.

7. See Walther Rehm, "Römisch–französischer Barockheroismus und seine Umgestaltung in Deutschland," *Germanisch–Romanische Monatsschrift*, Vol. XXII (1934); also, Willi Flemming, *Der Wandel des deutschen Naturgefühls vom 15. zum 18. Jahrhundert* (Halle, 1931).

8. *Versuch einer Critischen Dichtkunst* (Leipzig, 1751), p. 111.

9. *Dichtkunst*, p. 369.

10. *Critische Abhandlung von der Natur, den Absichten und dem Gebrauche der Gleichnisse* (Zürich, 1740), p. 221 f.

11. Vol. II, p. xviii.

12. Vol. XXXVI, pp. i, xxiii. It is interesting to check the *Allgemeine Deutsche Biographie* (1884), which bestowed glowing recognition on Bodmer and Breitinger in the articles about their careers; it adhered faithfully to their opinions on Lohenstein. This line persists almost word for word through the Merker–Stammler *Reallexicon der deutschen Literaturgeschichte* (1925; 1955), Wilhelm Kosch's *Deutsches Literatur–Lexicon* (1950), and many more handbooks.

13. *Das schlesische Kunstdrama* (Copenhagen, 1940), p. 183.

14. *Germanic Review*, X (1935), 227.

15. *Ibid.*, X, 225, 229.

16. *Dramatische Technik und Sprache in den Trauerspielen D. Caspers von Lohenstein* (Greifswald, 1911), p. 5.

17. *Der Stil in den Dramen Lohensteins* (Leipzig, 1927), p. 25.

18. *Zur Weltanschauung Daniel Caspars von Lohenstein* (Breslau, 1933), p. 31.

19. "Das 'Grosse Gemüt' im Drama Lohensteins," *Literaturwissenschaftliches Jahrbuch der Görres–Gesellschaft*, VIII (1936), 84, 89.

20. *Das Tragische in Lohensteins Trauerspielen* ("Wege zur Dichtung," Vol. XIV [1945]), pp. 80, 111, 117, 122.

21. "Lohensteins Sophonisbe als geschichtliche Tragödie," *Germanisch–Romanische Monatsschrift*, XXIX (1941), 27 f.

22. *Die Trauerspiele Lohensteins* ("Philologische Studien und Quellen," No. 9 [Berlin, 1961]), chap. v.

Chapter Two

23. We shall discuss in more detail, with regard to the African plays, Just's theory of two "energies" (love and politics) advanced in *Die Trauerspiele Lohensteins*; and indicate how Just oversimplifies when applying these categories. He does not interpret *I. B.*; however, the "energies" appear subordinate to the arcane level of fate even in this early play.

24. Lohenstein does not carry out this theme of endangerment as, for example, Hebbel later develops it in *Agnes Bernauer* or Grillparzer in *Die Jüdin von Toledo;* nevertheless, these nineteenth-century dramatists have their antecedents in the Spanish golden age and Elizabethan historical drama, and thus indirectly Lohenstein anticipates them.

Chapter Three

25. During this period, Lohenstein wrote one other dramatic work, his *Cleopatra* (1661), which he later revised and republished (1680) with *Sophonisbe.* We shall discuss the plays of 1680 as works developed beyond the *Agrippina* and as expressions of a matured playwright, since the versions of *Cleopatra* indicate a definite progression. *Ibrahim Sultan* (1673) represents, in contrast to the African histories, an intervening depression.

26. "Drama und Theater des deutschen Barock," *Zeitschrift für Deutschkunde,* XLVII (1935), 463.

27. M. O. Katz, *Zur Weltanschauung,* pp. 34 f., sees another source of ambiguity in what he considers to be Epicharis' mixed motivation; she is not a pure freedom martyr because also impelled by *personal* hatred of Nero and Neronian corruption.

28. Lunding, *Das schlesische Kunstdrama,* pp. 119, 122, counters such a view; he sees great merit in *Epicharis* as a drama of conspiracy and lauds Lohenstein's ironic elevation above his subject. This is the best interpretation of the play.

29. Fate is, nevertheless, so recondite (II, 576–80) that we must reject the definition by Schaufelberger, *Das Tragische in L.s Trauerspielen,* p. 112, that it has nothing in common with a higher power but is rather mere historical causality.

30. Just, *Die Trauerspiele Lohensteins,* p. 147, concludes: "Die Tragik der Epicharis liegt darin, dass sie unbeabsichtiger erotischer Wirkungen wegen in ihren geplanten politischen Aktionen zunächst Erfolg hat und dann scheitert." That she exercises strong erotic influence and suffers on that account is an exaggeration, unwarranted in view of the many interwoven events which contribute to the conspiracy's collapse, and to Epicharis' martyrdom, both directly and indirectly; Lohenstein is profounder than Just implies.

31. Compare Lunding, *op. cit.,* p. 127.

32. *Epicharis* exhibits the harshest Elizabethan naturalism, far removed from the "pure humanity" of German classicism exemplified in Goethe's *Iphigenie auf Tauris;* the bridge between these extremes is represented by dramas like Lessing's *Emilia Galotti,* with its *virtual* suicide to escape tyranny. Muris, *Dramatische Technik und Sprache,* p. 55, complains typically of the combination of sensualism and brutality in Lohenstein's dungeon scenes, of the heroine's suicide as "unnatural," "tasteless."

Chapter Four

33. The following chapters will touch on the myth of a golden rule under German aegis, the role of the Germans as expounded in the polyhistoric novel *Arminius* (Leipzig, 1689–90) and as revealed by the fifth chorus of *Cleopatra* and the Dido apparition of *Sophonisbe*.

34. Just, *Die Trauerspiele Lohensteins*, p. 59, interprets the opening speech as factual confirmation of the prince's supreme position, Nero's self-description as highest reality from the perspective of "baroque maximalism," rather than as dramatic irony.

35. Schaufelberger, *Das Tragische in L.s Trauerspielen*, pp. 84 ff., interprets the tyrant, in contrast to the martyr, as a person threatened not from without but from within—which applies clearly in the cases of Nero and Ibrahim Sultan.

36. See Julius Rütsch, *Das dramatische Ich im deutschen Barocktheater* ("Wege zur Dichtung," Vol. XII [1932]), 153 ff., on this genre as "pure theatre."

37. Just, *Die Trauerspiele Lohensteins*, p. 153, notes that Epicharis visualizes herself in a possible tragedy at the start of the drama, and interprets herself, but he does not connect this with the Genesius or Philemon theme of Jesuit drama, stressed by Rütsch as "transcendental irony" (pp. 168 ff., 182 ff.), nor cite other examples.

38. Compare the opinion of Lunding, *Das schlesische Kunstdrama*, p. 128, that there is no Rousseauistic attempt to escape courtly civilization, the real nexus of existence from which the figures cannot dissociate themselves.

39. *Das Tragische in L.s Trauerspielen*, p. 87.

40. *Das dramatische Ich*, p. 191.

41. *Das dramatische Ich*, p. 193.

Chapter Five

42. As a supplement to data given in Hans von Müller, "Bibliographie der Schriften L.s," see Edward Verhofstadt, "Zur Datierung der Urfassung von Lohensteins Cleopatra," *Neophilologus*, Vol. XLIV (1960). Conrad Müller, *Beiträge zum Leben und Dichten D. C.s von Lohenstein* (Breslau, 1882), pp. 72 ff., spends the larger part of his monograph in an analysis of *Cleopatra* and comparison of the two versions. The first critic who recognized the play's merits was August Kerkhoffs, *D. C. von Lohensteins Trauerspiele* (Paderborn, 1877); noting the changes in the second version, he felt they blunted its force in the last act. Both of these early apologists for *Cleopatra* ignored *Sophonisbe* as an inferior play, and their tendencies were still strong in Walter Martin, *Der Stil in den Dramen Lohensteins*, who made numerous

comparisons of the two versions of *Cl.* (pp. 27 ff.), discussed the other plays, but dismissed *So.* with a short negative judgment.

43. Lunding, *Das schlesische Kunstdrama*, p. 115, says similarly that Anthony denies the vital urge by adherence to a personal truth—in contrast to the masked, Machiavellian statesman figure.

44. See Just, *Die Trauerspiele Lohensteins*, chap. ii ("Sprache"), pp. 66 ff., on sententiousness, the interplay between fact and abstraction, and "das dichte sprachliche Bezugssystem" (p. 75)—what I call rhetorical proliferation. While noting an anticipatory function in much of Lohenstein's rhetoric, Just does not examine the ironic function.

45. Kerkhoffs, p. 27, notes as early proof of blindness Anthony's defense of Cleopatra's conduct at Actium.

46. Lunding, p. 156, views the ghosts and report, like everything weird or exotic in Lohenstein, as a mere "effect number." With greater justification, Kerkhoffs, pp. 52 f., finds that these ghostly happenings are integral to the dramatic action; he compares Shakespeare's usage in *Macbeth* or *Richard III* and even sees a Shakespearean sort of curse. He could also have referred (more precisely) to *Antony and Cleopatra*, V, iii, where a soldier interprets the occurrence: " 'Tis the god, Hercules, whom Anthony lov'd, / Now leaves him."

47. Günther Müller, *Deutsche Dichtung von der Renaissance bis zum Ausgang des Barock* (Wildpark–Potsdam, 1929), p. 241, concludes that Lohenstein's figures have their existence independent of transcendental standards: "the belief in absolute values withdraws into the aesthetic." This would certainly apply to Anthony's stature through *beautiful actions*.

48. Kerkhoffs, pp. 62 f., while receptive to the "Anthonian" phase of *Cleopatra* and to the well-drawn personalities in Augustus' party, regards the fourth and fifth acts as too broad, too detailed, weakening plot unity and climax; he expects a sentimental rather than historical development (Lohenstein's larger objective).

49. Cf. Lunding, p. 113.

50. Cf. Schaufelberger, *Das Tragische in L.s Trauerspielen*, p. 101.

51. Just, *Die Trauerspiele Lohensteins*, pp. 156 ff.

52. Lunding, p. 113; Oskar Nuglisch, *Barocke Stilelemente*, p. 55; Just, *Die Trauerspiele Lohensteins*, p. 160.

53. Martin, p. 29.

54. Cf. Kerkhoffs, pp. 70 f.

55. Which Kerkhoffs, pp. 70 f., and Lunding, p. 158, scorn as scholarship, not art; Oswald Muris, *Dramatische Technik und Sprache*, p. 44, acknowledges this as operatic pomp, satisfying both ear and eye, and gives other excellent examples of ceremonial moments (Sophonisbe's marriage, conjuring of Dido, coronation of Ibrahim Sultan's heir, etc.).

56. Cf. Kerkhoffs, pp. 73, 76.

Chapter Six

57. See Hans von Müller, "Bibliographie der Schriften D. C.s von Lohenstein," pp. 229–34. Concerning an eye-witness account of a performance of *Sophonisbe* in May, 1669, at the gymnasium of St. Maria Magdalena in Breslau (diary of Rector Major), see Max Hippe, "Aus dem Tagebuch eines Breslauer Schulmannes im 17. Jahrhundert," *Zeitschrift des Vereins für Geschichte und Altertum Schlesiens*, Vol. XXXVI (1902).

58. Wolfgang Kayser, "Lohensteins *Sophonisbe* als geschichtliche Tragödie," p. 32.

59. The "war of love" was a theme derived from antiquity (e.g., Ovid); the motif of love in militant harness is familiar throughout the seventeenth century, as in Kasper Stieler's *Geharnschte Venus* (1660).

60. Martin, *Der Stil in den Dramen Lohenstein*, p. 26.

61. Kayser, p. 25.

62. Nuglisch, *Barocke Stilelemente*, p. 57.

63. Muris, p. 36; Schaufelberger, *Das Tragische in L.s Trauerspielen*, p. 44; Laetitia Brede, "Das 'Grosse Gemüt' im Drama Lohensteins," p. 95.

64. Lunding, *Das schlesische Kunstdrama*, p. 104, sees Sophonisbe too exclusively as a superb actress on the world stage who seduces Masanissa in order to save her people but does not love him, although to win him over she deceives her own husband. Schaufelberger, p. 96, falls into the similar error of believing that Sophonisbe, like Cleopatra, overcomes her true love for the sake of personal survival; without unconditional identity, her existence sinks to a mere role. The opposite is true, for Sophonisbe accepts even the moral contradictions in her behavior in order to find her queenly identity (Dido).

65. Pp. 425 ff., 428.

66. Kayser, p. 32, gives the best summary of this stature as a magnanimous heroine; heroic in the manner she accepts destiny, the queen is, however, only finally great because she has striven for a great goal, to save her realm.

67. Cf. Nuglisch, pp. 35, 37.

Chapter Seven

68. See his excellent essay "Der europäische Barock," in *Der Dichter und die Zeit* (Bern, 1947). For a wider perspective and survey of the fine arts, consult Victor-L. Tapié, *The Age of Grandeur: Baroque Art and Architecture* (New York, 1960), which appeared in the original French as *Baroque et Classicisme* (Paris, 1957); especially the first chapter, "The Birth of the Baroque," corrects the exaggerated separation of Renaissance from baroque.

69. P. Feit, *Sophonisbe in Geschichte und Dichtung* (Lübeck, 1888); Charles Ricci, *Sophonisbe dans la tragédie classique italienne et française* (Torino, 1904); A. Andrae, *Sophonisbe in der französischen Tragödie, mit Berücksichtigung der Sophonisbe–Bearbeitungen in anderen Literaturen* (1891); A. J. Axelrad, *Le thème de Sophonisbe dans les principales tragédies de la littérature occidentale* (Lille, 1956); Gerhard Saupe, *Die Sophonisbe-tragödien der englischen Literatur des 17. und 18. Jahrhunderts* (Osterwieck am Harz, 1929); S. Vrancken, *Das Antonius–Cleopatra–Motiv in der deutschen Literatur* (Bonn, 1930); Georg Hermann Möller, *Beiträge zur dramatischen Cleopatra–Literatur* (Schweinfurt, 1907) [contains numerous errors].

70. On the relations between Italian and English literature, consult the collection of essays by Mario Praz, *The Flaming Heart* (New York, 1958), especially "The Politic Brain: Machiavelli and the Elizabethans." For the French seventeenth century, consult Jean Rousset, *La littérature de l'âge baroque en France* (Paris, 1953).

71. An invaluable book treating the *history* of classical and vernacular prosody (Greek, Latin, Norse, Celtic, Germanic, English, and Romance) is W. P. Ker's *The Dark Ages* (New York, 1958). "[The Dark Ages'] end is marked by the appearance of the new Romance languages and their poetry, which take captive the Teutonic countries, and destroy the chances of the old Teutonic manner of composing verse. The Teutonic fashions are displaced on their own ground. No Teutonic verse is so near to modern English poetry as the Provençal measures are. When Wordsworth imitates the stanza of Burns he is really imitating William of Poitou, who used it seven hundred years earlier . . . " (p. 15). Blank verse, for example, is as much a Romance form as is the alexandrine.

72. In addition to Just, see Paul Stachel, *Seneca und das deutsche Renaissancedrama* ("Palaestra," Vol. XLVI [1907]), 282–324, on Lohenstein.

73. The best single work giving the history of the theater in the seventeenth century is the third volume (*Das Theater der Barockzeit*) of Heinz Kindermann's monumental *Theatergeschichte Europas* (Salzburg, 1959). Part six, "Das Barocktheater in Deutschland, Österreich und der Schweiz," treats the influence and activities of the English, Dutch, Italian, and German wandering troupes, the opera, Jesuit drama, the imperial theatrical culture of the Austrian sphere, and Protestant school drama (pp. 349–562). For an examination of the complicated subject of the Breslau theater, to which Gryphius and Lohenstein contributed, readers should consult especially section c, "Protestantisches Schultheater: Staatstragödie und Typenkomödie." Kindermann approaches the evidence, carefully assembled, without any preconceived literary expectations and documents this rich moment in the German past; his notations of secondary literature (pp. 651–59) and specialized bibliography (pp. 679–88) are the most complete sources available. Because he describes in detail the actual stage practices of Gryphian and Lohensteinian style, his interpretation of such matters as "bombast," "alternation technique," "illusionary stage effects," etc., is absolutely necessary reading in order to counterbalance analyses from a purely literary standpoint. The picture of a deep stage with intricate, often mobile props, extensive machinery, and highly developed lighting techniques makes understandable many of the peculiarities of humanistic *school* drama under certain late Romance influences; rather than there being some distortion or discrepancy

between the rhetorical pathos of the actors and a sober environment of philosophy, there was the closest connection between the heroic complaint against "transitoriness" in a world theater and the actual performance of plays on a "Verwandlungsbühne"—whose moods were created with use of curtains, divisions of horizontal and vertical space, music, sound and light effects in skilful fluctuations.

74. As Kindermann notes in his "Schlusswort" to Vol. III, p. 634, and examines in Part 1, "Französisches Theater zwischen Barock und Klassik," of Vol. IV (1961), the twentieth century has also rediscovered the *French* baroque drama, which flourished side by side with the emerging neo-classical style that was to triumph toward the eighteenth century. In fact, of course, great theatrical geniuses like Corneille and Molière were able to participate in both of these distinct streams of style, which the French public apparently was able to enjoy contemporaneously. In addition, consult Rousset for a re-evaluation of the "contest" between baroque and classicism.

Bibliography

BIBLIOGRAPHY

THIS LISTING does not repeat all titles cited in the footnotes. It is limited to discussions of Lohenstein's plays, a restricted number of studies touching German seventeenth-century drama, and a few general references. The interested reader can find topically arranged bibliographies for Lohenstein's age in Richard Newald's *Die deutsche Literatur vom Späthumanismus zur Empfindsamkeit, 1570–1750 (Geschichte der deutschen Literatur*, ed. H. DeBoor and R. Newald, Vol. V [3rd rev. ed.; Munich, 1951]), and in Hans von Müller, "Bibliographie der Schriften Lohensteins," *Werden und Werken: Festgruss für K. W. Hiersemann* (Leipzig, 1924).

I. *Lohenstein's Works*

Arminius. Leipzig, 1689–90.

Cleopatra. Breslau, 1661.

"Collection A 1." Breslau, 1680. Containing *Cleopatra, Sophonisbe, Blumen, Geistliche Gedancken,* etc., the most complete gathering of diverse pieces by Lohenstein's original publisher, Fellgibel.

Türkische Trauerspiele, Römische Trauerspiele, and *Africanische Trauerspiele,* ed. KLAUS GÜNTHER JUST ("Bibliothek des Literarischen Vereins in Stuttgart," Nos. 292–94). Stuttgart, 1953–57.

II. *Works on Lohenstein's Drama*

BREDE, LAETITIA. "Das 'Grosse Gemüt' im Drama Lohensteins," *Literatur wissenschaftliches Jahrbuch der Görres–Gesellschaft,* Vol. VIII (1936).

JUST, KLAUS GÜNTHER. *Die Trauerspiele Lohensteins, Versuch einer Interpretation* ("Philologische Studien und Quellen," No. 9). Berlin, 1961.

KAMIL, BURHANEDDIN. *Die Türken in der deutschen Literatur bis zum Barock und die Sultansgestalten in den Türkendramen Lohensteins.* Kiel, 1935.

KATZ, MAX OTTO. *Zur Weltanschauung Daniel Caspars von Lohenstein.* Breslau, 1933.

KAYSER, WOLFGANG. "Lohensteins *Sophonisbe* als geschichtliche Tragödie," *Germanisch-Romanische Monatsschrift*, Vol. XXIX (1941).

KERKHOFFS, AUGUST. *Daniel Casper von Lohensteins Trauerspiele*. Paderborn, 1877.

LUBOS, A. "Das schlesische Barocktheater: Daniel Caspar von Lohenstein," *Jahrbuch der Schlesischen Friedrich-Wilhelms-Universität zu Breslau*, Vol. V (1960). Not seen by the author.

LUPTON, P. W. *Die Frauengestalten in den Trauerspielen Daniel Caspers von Lohenstein*. Wien, 1954. Not seen by the author.

MARTIN, WALTHER. *Der Stil in den Dramen Lohensteins*. Leipzig, 1927.

MÜLLER, CONRAD. *Beiträge zum Leben und Dichten D.C.s von Lohenstein* ("Germanistische Abhandlungen," Vol. I). Breslau, 1882.

MURIS, OSWALD. *Dramatische Technik und Sprache in den Trauerspielen D. Caspers von Lohenstein*. Greifswald, 1911.

PASSOW, W. A. *D.C. von Lohenstein, seine Trauerspiele und seine Sprache*. Meiningen, 1852.

SCHAUFELBERGER, FRITZ. *Das Tragische in Lohensteins Trauerspielen* ("Wege zur Dichtung," Vol. XLV). 1945.

VERHOFSTADT, EDWARD. *Daniel Casper von Lohenstein: Untergehende Wertwelt und ästhetischer Illusionismus* ("Veröffentlichungen der Philosophischen Fakultät Gent," Vol. CXXXIII). Brügge, 1964. Not seen by the author.

―――. "Zur Datierung der Urfassung von Lohensteins *Cleopatra*," *Neophilologus*, Vol. XLIV (1960).

III. Studies of Baroque Drama

ALEWYN, RICHARD. "Der Geist des Barocktheaters," in *Weltliteratur: Festgabe für Fritz Strich zum 70. Geburtstag*. Bern, 1952.

BENJAMIN, WALTER. *Ursprung des deutschen Trauerspiels*. Berlin, 1928.

BOBERTAG, FELIX. "Die deutsche Kunsttragödie des 17. Jahrhunderts," *Archiv für Literaturgeschichte*, Vol. V (1876).

BRATES, G. *Hauptprobleme der deutschen Barockdramaturgie*. Rostock, 1935.

FLEMMING, WILLI. "Das deutsche Barockdrama und die Politik," *Euphorion (Dichtung und Volkstum)*, Vol. XXXVII (1936).

―――. "Drama und Theater des deutschen Barock," *Zeitschrift für Deutschkunde* (1935).

―――. "Die Erfassung des Epochalstils barocker Schauspielkunst," *Maske und Kothurn*, Vol. I (1955).

FRIEDERICH, WERNER PAUL. "From Ethos to Pathos: The Development from Gryphius to Lohenstein," *Germanic Review*, Vol. X (1935).

HAERTEN, HEINZ. *Vondel und der deutsche Barock* ("Disquisitiones Carolinae," Vol. V). 1934,

HAMMES, FRITZ. *Das Zwischenspiel im deutschen Drama von seinen Anfängen bis auf Gottsched.* Berlin, 1911.

HILDEBRANDT, HEINRICH. *Die Staatsauffassung der schlesischen Barockdramatiker im Rahmen ihrer Zeit.* Rostock, 1939.

IBLHER, F. W. *Der Dramatische Stil des 17. Jahrhunderts.* München, 1922.

KINDERMANN, HEINZ. *Theatergeschichte Europas.* Vol. III. Salzburg, 1959.

LUNDING, ERIK. *Das Schlesische Kunstdrama, eine Darstellung und eine Deutung.* Copenhagen, 1940.

MEINHARDT, HELMUT. *Stoffe, Ideen und Motive im schlesischen Kunstdrama des 17. Jahrhunderts.* Rostock, 1925.

MONATH, WOLFGANG. *Das Motiv der Selbsttötung in der deutschen Tragödie des 17. und frühen 18. Jahrhunderts.* Würzburg, 1956.

NUGLISCH, OSKAR. *Barocke Stilelemente in der dramatischen Kunst von A. Gryphius und D. C. von Lohenstein* ("Sprache und Kultur der Germanischen und Romanischen Völker, Germanistische Reihe," Vol. XXX). Breslau, 1938.

POPP, GEORG. *Uber den Begriff des Dramas in den deutschen Poetiken des 17. Jahrhunderts.* Leipzig, 1895.

REHM, WALTHER. "Römisch–französischer Barockheroismus und seine Umgestaltung in Deutschland," *Germanisch–Romanische Monatsschrift,* Vol. XXII (1934).

REISS, WALTER. *Die Theorie des Tragischen im 17. Jahrhundert in Deutschland und Frankreich.* Bern, 1907.

RÜTSCH, JULIUS. *Das dramatische Ich im deutschen Barocktheater* ("Wege zur Dichtung," Vol. XII). 1932.

SCHILD, K. A. *Die Bezeichnungen der deutschen Dramen von den Anfängen bis 1740.* Giessen, 1925.

SEXAU, RICHARD. *Der Tod im deutschen Drama des 17. und 18. Jahrhunderts.* Bern, 1906.

STACHEL, PAUL. *Seneca und das deutsche Renaissance Drama* ("Palaestra," Vol. XLVI). 1907.

STRICH, FRITZ. "Das europaische Barock," in *Der Dichter und die Zeit.* Bern, 1947.

WENTZLAFF–EGGEBERT, FRIEDRICH–WILHELM. "Die deutsche Barocktragödie: zur Funktion von 'Glaube' und 'Vernunft' im Drama des 17. Jahrhunderts, *Formkräfte der deutschen Dichtung vom Barock bis zur Gegenwart.* Göttingen, 1962.

IV. *Works on English Comedians,
the Popular Stage, and the
Renaissance Theater*

ALEWYN, RICHARD. "Schauspieler und Stegreifbühne des Barock," in *Mimus und Logos: Festgabe für Carl Niessen.* Emsdetten, 1952.

BAESECKE, ANNA. *Das Schauspiel der englischen Komödianten in Deutschland.* Halle, 1935.

BOLTE, J. *Die Singspiele der englishchen Komödianten.* Hamburg, 1893.

BORCHERDT, HANS-HEINRICH. "Der Renaissancestil des Theaters," in *Die Ernte. Abhandlungen zur Literaturwissenschaft. Franz Muncker zu seinem 70. Geburtstag ürberreicht.* Halle, 1926.

BRÜNNING, IDA. *Le théâtre en Allemagne, son origine et ses luttes (1200–1760).* Paris, 1887.

COHN, A. *Shakespeare in Germany in the Sixteenth and Seventeenth Centuries.* N.p., 1865.

HEINE, CARL. *Das Schauspiel der deutschen Wanderbühne vor Gottsched.* Halle, 1889.

KUTSCHER, A. "Die Commedia dell' Arte und Deutschland," *Die Schaubühne,* Vol. XLIII (1955).

REULING, C. *Die Komische Figur in den wichtigsten deutschen Dramen bis zum Ende des XVII. Jahrhunderts.* N.p., 1890.

RICHTER, W. *Liebeskampf 1630 und Schaubühne 1670. Ein Beitrag zur deutschen Theatergeschichte des 17. Jahrhunderts.* Berlin, 1910.

V. Works on Jesuit Drama

ADEL, KURT. *Das Jesuitendrama in Österreich.* Wien, 1957.

BECHER, HUBERT. "Die geistige Entwicklungsgeschichte des Jesuitendramas," *Deutsche Vierteljahrsschrift,* Vol. XIX (1941).

FLEMMING, WILLI. *Geschichte des Jesuitentheaters in den Landen deutscher Zunge.* Berlin, 1923.

HAPP, ALFRED. *Die Dramentheorie der Jesuiten.* München, 1923.

MÜLLER, JOHANNES. *Das Jesuitendrama in den Ländern deutscher Zunge.* Augsburg, 1930.

PFANDL, LUDWIG. "Einführung in die Literatur des Jesuitendramas in Deutschland," *Germanisch–Romanische Monatsschrift,* Vol. II (1910).

SCHEID, NIKOLAUS, S. J. "Das lateinische Jesuitendrama im deutschen Sprachgebiet," *Literaturwissenschaftliches Jahrbuch der Görres–Gesellschaft,* Vol. V (1930).

VI. General Reference Works

BENZ, RICHARD. *Deutsches Barock.* Vol. I. Stuttgart, 1949.

CROCE, BENEDETTO. *Der Begriff des Barock—Die Gegenreformation.* Zurich, 1925.

CYSARZ, HERBERT. *Deutsche Barockdichtung.* Leipzig, 1924.

————. "Vom Geiste des deutschen Literatur–Barocks," *Deutsche Vierteljahrsschrift*, Vol. I (1923).

ERMATINGER, EMIL. *Barock und Rokoko*. Leipzig, 1928.

FLEMMING, WILLI. *Deutsche Kultur im Zeitalter des Barock*. Potsdam, 1937–39.

————. *Das Jahrhundert des Barock, 1600–1700*. Stuttgart, 1952.

————. *Der Wandel des deutschen Naturgefuhls vom 15. zum 18. Jahrhundert*. Halle, 1931.

HANKAMER, PAUL. *Deutsche Gegenreformation und deutsches Barock* (*Epochen der deutschen Literatur*, Vol. II, Pt. 2). Stuttgart, 1935.

HECKEL, H. *Geschichte der deutschen Literatur in Schlesien*. Breslau, 1929.

HÜBSCHER, ARTHUR. "Barock als Gestaltung antithetischen Lebensgefühls," *Euphorion*, Vol. XXIV (1922).

————. "Das Problem der geistesgeschichtlichen Pseudomorphose in Renaissance und Barock," *Euphorion*, Vol. XXVI (1924).

LUDERS, E. *Die Auffassung des Menschen im 17. Jahrhundert*. Köln, 1935.

MÜLLER, GÜNTHER. *Deutsche Dichtung von der Renaissance bis zum Ausgang des Barock*. Wildpark–Potsdam, 1927–29.

————. *Höfische Kultur der Barockzeit* (*Höfische Kultur*, ed. HANS NAUMANN and GÜNTHER MÜLLER). Halle, 1929.

————. "Die Wende vom Barock zur Aufklärung," *Literaturwissenschaftliches Jahrbuch der Görres–Gesellschaft*, Vol. VIII (1936).

MÜLLER, RICHARD. *Dichtung und bildende Kunst im Zeitalter des deutschen Barock* ("Wege zur Dichung," Vol. XXVIII). N.p., 1937.

STAMMLER, WOLFGANG. *Von der Mystik zum Barock*. Vol. II, Pt. 1. 2nd ed. Stuttgart, 1950.

TRUNZ, ERICH. "Weltbild und Dichtung im deutschen Barock," in *Aus der Welt des Barocks*. Stuttgart, 1957.

VIËTOR, KARL. *Probleme der deutschen Barockliteratur*. Leipzig, 1928.

————. "Vom Stil und Geist der deutschen Barockdichtung," *Germanisch–Romanische Monatsschrift*, Vol. XIV (1926).

————. "Das Zeitalter des Barock," *Zeitschrift für Deutschkunde* (1928).

VOGT, ERIKA. *Die gegenhöfische Strömung in der deutschen Barockliteratur*. Leipzig, 1932.

WEISBACH, WERNER. *Der Barock als Kunst der Gegenreformation*. Berlin, 1921.

————. "Barock als Stilphänomen," *Deutsche Vierteljahrsschrift*, Vol. II (1924).

WELLEK, ALBERT. "Renaissance– und Barock–Synästhesie. Die Geschichte des Doppelempfindens im 16. und 17. Jahrhundert," *Deutsche Vierteljahrsschrift*, Vol. IX (1931).

WÖLFFLIN, HEINRICH. *Renaissance und Barock*. München, 1907.

Bibliographical Addendum

SCHÖNE, ALBRECHT. *Emblematik und Drama im Zeitalter des Barock.* München, 1964. This book was not obtainable in time for consideration in the text or notes, which had gone to press, but merits special mention for its significant contribution to the understanding of German seventeenth-century drama generally, and Lohenstein's language in particular; Schöne's analyses of baroque theatre in the light of emblematic procedures are truly outstanding.

Index

INDEX

Absolute rule, 47, 76, 131

Absolutism, v, 29; age of, 90

Accademia della Crusca, 10

Achmat, 31, 32, 36

Acte, 62

Actium, n. 45; defeat of, 86

Aeneas, 57–58, 133–34; story of Dido and, 113

Africa, 121, 133, 135, 143; choral personification of, 45

African materials, 111

African plays, 45, 79, 130, 142, 152, nn. 1, 23, 25

African queens, 26

"Afterplay," 55

Agrippina, 21, 41, 53, 58–73, 77, 81–82, 94, 101, 103, 116, 119, 149–51; as Cartesian animal, 70; beauty of, 150; fall of, 69; ghost of, 73; incestuous behavior of, 64; role of, 66; shipwreck of, 66

Agrippina, 5, 43, 56, 58, 61, 63, 72, 73, 83, 92, 96, 98, 113, 115, 117, 134, 150, 151, n. 24; choruses in, 56; incest in, 63; love in, 62

Alcmaeon, 73

Alexander the Great, 81, 107

Alexandria, 86, 101

Alexandrine, n. 71; French, 11, 147; German, 147

Ambition, 114, 128

Ambre, 39–41, 49, 58, 74, 78, 151; ghost of, 78; love pact with Begler-Beg, 40–41; suicide of, 40; violation of, 39–40

America, 143, 147

Amilcar, 117

Amurat, ghost of, 74

Anacreontic mode, 6

Andrae, A., n. 69

Anicetus, 70

Anthony, 36, 81–104, 107, 109, 112, 115, 130, 138, 141, 151, nn. 43, 45, 47; burial of, 104, 106; consciousness of history of, 83; death of, 98, 100–101; dream of, 97; dual nature of, 98; fall of, 91; marriage to Octavia, 90; removal of, 82; role of, 99; self-destruction of, 97, 99; victims of (Antigonus, Artabazes, Jamblichus), 97

Antihero, 34, 38, 42–44, 72, 150; antiheroic behavior, 41; antiheroic monster, 35; antiheroic type, 81; antiheroism, 26

Antony and Cleopatra; see Shakespeare

Antyllus, 81–82, 107

Archibius, 88

Arminius, 5, 17, 108, 143, nn. 2, 33

Asia, 143; personification of, 29, 33–34

Assyrian empire, 141

Astarth, 122

Augustus, 81, 84, 86–87, 92–95, 100–104, 106–8, 126, 128, 139; emissary of, 82, 90; feigned passion of, 102–3; Machiavellian statecraft, morality, and reverence of, 102; role of, 108; trap of, 94

Austria, ruling house of, 108, 141; Austrian court, 4; Austrian rule, 143

Avancini, Nikolaus, 13

Axelrad, A. J., n. 69

Ayrer, Jakob, 13

Bacchus, 98

Bach, Johann Sebastian, 18

Baroque (*Barock*), v, 71, 128, 145, nn. 34, 68, 74

"Beautiful soul," 69

Beauty, 9, 23, 38, 40, 62, 90, 129, 130, 140, 142 150; divine origin of, 150; nihilistically attuned, 98; of earth, 132; of woman, 141

Beaux sentiments, 106

Begler-Beg, 74

Biderman, Jakob, 13

Blank verse, 11, n. 71

Bobertag, Felix, 19

Bodmer, Johann Jakob, 16–17, 19, 138

Böckman, Paul, n. 6

Böhme, Jakob, 7, 9, 26

Bogudes, 122–23; priesthood of, 124

Bondage: earthly, 50; in time, 105; natural, 49; passionate, 91

Brede, Laetitia, 23–24, 133, n. 63

Breitinger, Johan Jakob, 16–17, 19

Breslau, 3–4, 10, n. 57

Britannicus, ghost of, 72

Burns, Robert, n. 71

Burrhus, 62, 73

Caesar, Julius, 94–95, 98, 102, 104

Caesarion, 89, 102

Caesars, descent of house of, 58

Calderón de la Barca, Pedro, 146; *La Vida es sueño,* 76; theodicy of, 76

Calvinism, 78

Cassidius, 87

Caracalla, Bassianus, 43–44

Cartesian thought, 7, 9; universe, 130

Carthage, 112, 115, 135, 141; Carthaginian civilization, 117–18; Carthaginian episode, 112; Carthaginian role, 113

Catharina, 30

Catharsis, 12

Christianity, 5, 10, 21, 22, 34; Christian beliefs, 152; death wish, 32; faith, 33; miracle, 153; notion of blessed isolation, 51; pessimism, 130–31; traditions, 149

Civilization, courtly, 16, n. 38

Classicism, 148, n. 74; French national, 146-47; German, 22, n. 32

Classicistic play, 126

Cleopatra, 21, 23, 25, 53, 66, 71, 81–107, 109, 111–12, 116–17, 119, 141, 149, 151, 152, n. 64; beauty of, 81, 92; burial ceremony of, 96; death of, 81; feigned suicide of, 95–96, 99, 100; monologue of, 92; rationality of, 93; role of, 82–83, 92, 95–96, 103–5, 151; suicide of, 103, 151; tragedy of, 93; world of, 96

Cleopatra, 5, 19, 23, 27, 36, 73, 83, 86, 92–93, 100, 109, 111–16, 122, 126, 136, 139, 141, nn. 3, 33, 42, 48; expansion of, 81; versions of, 81, 111, 140, n. 25

Cléopâtre (*Rodogune*), 124, 130, 146

Cléopâtre (Jodelle), 145

Commedia dell' arte, 14

Concettismo, 6

Conscience, 29, 39, 56, 72, 94, 119, 129

Corneille, Pierre, 4, 15, 53, 147, n. 74; category of admiration, 91; category of compassion, 91; *Rodogune,* 124, 130, 146

Counter Reformation, 10, 12

Court, 31, 42, 62, 65; of Louis XIV, 62

Critischer Musikus, 18

Cyrtha: burning of, 113; fall of, 114

Cysarz, Herbert (*Deutsche Barock-Dichtung*), 19–20

Cythera, embarkation for, 99

Danube, personification of, 108

Dark Ages, 146

Death (*Tod*), 33–34, 36, 40, 44, 50–52, 60, 63–64, 68–70, 78, 85, 87–89, 95–97, 99, 103, 105, 107, 123, 131–32, 136, 140, 141, 149; as fixer of roles, 99; sacrificial, 98

Decameron, 13

Deity, beneficent, 108; Christian, 40

Desengaño, 50, 131

Destiny, 26, 47, 52, 65, 69, 73, 83, 86, 90, 92, 104, 112, 115, 120, 134, 143; consciousness of, 136; human, 45; seeds of, 58

Mozart, Wolfgang Amadeus, 134
Müller, Conrad, 23, n. 42
Müller, Günther, n. 47
Müller, Hans von, nn. 1, 42, 57
Müller, Helmut, n. 3
Muris, Oswald, 19, 23, 133, nn. 32, 55, 63

Nadler, J., 19
Narcisse, 59
Natalis, 47
Nature: animal, 38, 136; human, 49, 93; moral, 26, 62; personification of, 67–68; as symbolic theater, 67
Necessity: historical, 85, 101, 111; political, 90
Negativism, Lohenstein's, 27, 42
Nemesis, 27, 28, 69, 78, 95; play of, 83
Nero, 44, 46–47, 49–51, 56, 58–66, 69–70, 72–73, 75, nn. 27, 34, 35; soul of, 52, 72
Nihilism, erotic, 32, 147
Nile, personification of, 108
Nimptsch, 3
Nineteenth century, 130; dramatists of, n. 24
Nobility, 34, 36, 39, 46, 62; ethics of, 64; human, 48; personal, 91; role of, 115
North Africa, 112; culture of, 132
Novel, psychological, 64
Nuglisch, Oskar, 103, 128, nn. 52, 62

Octavia, 60, 62
Oedipus at Colonnus, 153
Oenone, 64
Opitz, Martin, 10–11; Buch von der deutschen Poeterey, 10
Order, 44, 45
Orestes, 73
Orient, 29
Osiris, 89, 98

Otho, 58, 59
Ottoman empire, 4

Pallas, 57–58, 117
Papinianus, 20, 43–44, 53, 128
Paris, 57–58, 91
Passion (Brunst), 7, 9, 21, 23, 25, 28–29, 35, 37–38, 49, 57–58, 62–64, 66–67, 70, 74, 88–89, 92, 104, 114, 117, 119, 122 126–27 150–52; enslavement of, 93; weapons of, 41, 66; world of, 66
Passion play, 12
Passow, W. A., 19
Pathos, 15, 20–22, 92, 123, 132; rhetorical, n. 6
Penthesilea, 117
Permanence, 39, 40, 90, 93, 152; extra-historical, 99
Pessimism, 33, 53, 74, 134
Petrarchistic mode, 6
Phébus, 148
Phèdre, 63, 69, 137
Philosophy: contemporary, 29; mechanistic, 27, 130; pre-Socratic, 137; rationalistic, 152
Phoenician civilization, 112, 122
Pietism, 5
Piso, 48
Play (Spiel), 114, 115; mystery, 12; "verrücktes Spiel der Zeit," 72, 94, 115
Pléiade, 11
Poetry, manneristic, 6: of Lohenstein, 7–8
Poppaea, 51, 58, 59, 61–63
Politics, 31, 46–47, 58, 60, 92–94, 119, 140, n. 5; Machiavellian, 130; realistic, 122
Posa, Marquis de, 39
Power, 23, 83, 86, 132, 150; philosophy of, 125; political, 29, 114; system of, 75
Praz, Mario, n. 70
Predestination, 72
Princesse de Clèves, 64